The Antediluvian Librarians'
Secrets for Success
in Seminary and Theology School

The Antediluvian Librarians'
Secrets for Success
in Seminary and Theology School

Jane Lenz Elder, Duane Harbin, and David Schmersal

Designed and Illustrated by Rebecca Howdeshell

Bridwell Press
Southern Methodist University
Dallas, TX
2022

Bridwell Press is the professional publishing arm of
Bridwell Library (SMU Libraries and Perkins School of Theology).

SMU. Libraries   SMU. Perkins

Manufactured in the United States of America

DOI: http://dio.org/10.3998/mpub.12686773
ISBN 978-1-95746-01-6 (paperback)
ISBN 978-1-95746-00-9 (open access)

To the students, past and present, of Perkins School of Theology.

About the Authors and Illustrator

Jane Lenz Elder is the Head of the Reference, Research, and Theological Writing Center at Bridwell Library, Perkins School of Theology, in Dallas, Texas. She holds graduate degrees in Theology, History, and Library Science, and has published several works on the history of the Southwestern United States and the American film industry. In private life, she and her husband are doting grandparents, and they revel in their pack of dogs, which includes Arthur, the Irish Wolfhound.

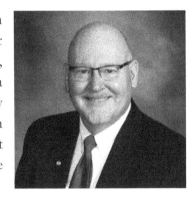

Now retired, Duane Harbin served at Perkins School of Theology in Dallas, Texas for more than 25 years, ending as Assistant Dean for Technology, Planning and Compliance. He holds degrees in Linguistics, Divinity, and Library Science and has been an active member of Atla since 1982 (when it was known as the American Theological Library Association). Duane devotes his spare time to his Pembroke Welsh Corgi, his nearly classic Thunderbird, and the Episcopal Church (not necessarily in that order). In his non-spare time, he studies the art of the "whodunit" and toys with idea of writing one.

David Schmersal is an Access and Instruction Librarian at Stitt Library, Austin Presbyterian Theological Seminary in Austin, Texas. He holds master's degrees in theology and library science. When not in the library, he may be found engaging in a Sisyphean effort to whittle down his ever-growing list of books to read, desperately trying to prevent even more of the Greek and Hebrew he learned in seminary from falling out of his head, stinging from the latest epic defeat his teenage son inflicted on him in Risk, enjoying the natural beauty of central Texas with his family, or cooking or cleaning *something*.

Rebecca Howdeshell has been an artist for over twenty years, a passion that has contributed to her love of artists' and other rare books. She has held the position of Digital Projects Librarian at Bridwell Library for twelve years, and is passionate about featuring the extraordinary collection of rare books, manuscripts, prints, and broadsides at Bridwell Library Special Collections online and through illustration. Rebecca lives in Dallas with her menagerie of pets and enjoys exploring exhibited art at museums and galleries, trying restaurants with friends and family, and finding every park in the Dallas area with her dog, Dinah.

Table of Contents

Foreword ....*i*

PART ONE: BEFORE YOU BEGIN, ORIENT YOURSELF *1*

  Ask for Help and You Shall Receive It 3

  Graduate School Differs from What You've Done Before 4

  In Praise of Stupid Questions 6

  Know Thyself 7

  And Know a Few Other Things, Too 9

  Books We Wish We Had Read before Coming to Seminary or Theology School 11

PART TWO: ONCE YOU HAVE BEGUN *13*

  Think Before You Buy 15

  Time Management 17

  Reading Strategically 18

  Effective Note-Taking 20

  Critical Thinking and Critical Humility 22

  Resources for Once You Have Begun 24

PART THREE: HABITS TO LAST A LIFETIME *25*

  The Myth of Multitasking 27

  Take Good Care of Yourself 29

  Cordial Discourse 31

  Comparisons Are Useless—You Do You 33

  Giving and Receiving Criticism 35

  Resources for Habits to Last a Lifetime 37

PART FOUR: THEOLOGICAL RESEARCH *39*

  Resources to Know About 41

  The Three Faces of Google 43

  Primary, Secondary, and Tertiary Sources 45

  What Footnotes and Bibliographies Are Trying to Tell Us 47

  Wikipedia: Love It or Hate It, but Don't Cite It 49

  Resources: Theological Research 51

PART FIVE: WRITING – GETTING IT ON PAPER *53*

  How Shall I Write Thee? Let Me Count the Ways 55

  Selecting a Topic and Crafting a Thesis 57

Introducing Structure 59

The Critical Importance of Lousy First Drafts 61

An Ode to Strunk & White 63

Resources: Our Favorite Books on Writing 64

PART SIX: WRITING MECHANICS-MAKING IT PRETTY AND CORRECT 65

Grammar, Spelling, and Punctuation 67

A Special Note on Apostrophes 69

Active vs. Passive Voice Verbs 71

My What Is Dangling? 73

Finishing Touches 74

Favorite Resources for Writing...76

Our Favorite Real-Life Spell Czech Misses 77

PART SEVEN: THE HARD STUFF..79

Pacing Yourself for Larger Papers 81

Scholarly Citations and Plagiarism 83

Preparing for Exams 85

Writer's Block...86

Creating an Organizational System for Life...88

Resources: Study Breaks and Personal Rewards 90

Appendix: Homework *92*

Acknowledgments..*94*

Foreword

"Don't bend; don't water it down; don't try to make it logical; don't edit your own soul according to the fashion. Rather, follow your most intense obsessions mercilessly." These are the words that have been falsely attributed to Franz Kafka for nearly a quarter century. They were in fact the words of the modern gothic novelist Anne Rice, who penned them in a 1995 preface to a newly republished collection of Kafka's stories and miscellany. Words, sentences, and writing itself are both an art and a science—we are given tools of precision to undertake an action, and rules to follow in order to make that action clear, communicable, and understood; yet it is in our own mental spheres to articulate something beautiful, transformative, even transcendent, or so we hope. When we write, though, we risk succumbing to the narratives of the day or those subsequent years that may confuse or blend or upset the reality of the language one writes—like attributing Anne Rice's words to Kafka: how Kafkan!

Consider that writing has origins not just in us, but among us and our environments. Good writing, especially, is hard to come by. It is an art that blossoms from the same "merciless obsessions" that Ms. Rice herself speaks of here, but obsession does not always good writing make! There is a subtle need to drive hard at revision, especially among the modern craftspersons of the articulated word, because as many writers, authors, and wordsmiths know, we can nearly always write things better with a little more finessing and editing. This also makes us recognize that writing is neither unilateral nor uniform in its content, style, or delivery, because even if there is one writer, there are many influences upon that writer, as well as editors, teachers, and publishers, who have populated the mental and real realms of that person. Furthermore, there are multitudes of literary categories and genres, of fiction, literature, non-fiction, creative prose, poetry, and whatnot. And there are a plethora of formulae, best practices by academic discipline, and an aggregated desire for consensus on how to write best in one area or another. Yet, there rarely is consensus, even in the days since the great "Samuels"—Johnson or Pepys—or more recently the venerable Strunk and White, the doyens and militant syntacticians of twentieth-century American English. Language and writing are evolving within the parameters of Latin's intractable legacy on English grammar.

Why can't we split infinitives? Blame Carlyle! Why can't we end a sentence with a preposition? Cicero would have chafed! Why mustn't we use the passive voice (which I find both deliciously poetic, and functionally useless and evasive, but which I admit to being a shameless employer)? Because it's a Nixonian vaguery! Rules are meant to guide us to help us communicate in ways that other people can understand what we are trying to convey, and in so doing, this helps with clarity and precision. We can sometime break those rules, but only when it serves a purpose, and when we understand the rules, or why those rules were implemented in the first place. In theological writing we find an excellent and unique example in the framing of thoughts and the articulation of language, because this kind of writing is an expansive expression of the human spirit that extends its poetics and prosaic wings, like Hegel's owl of Minerva, which only flies at dusk—a metaphor that for us means that we only fully understand our writing (and especially our theological writing) once we've completed it.

Jane Lenz Elder, Duane Harbin, and David Schmersal have presented us with a timely and most useful work that stands out in this genre and category of writing. As Minerva's owl takes flight in the dusk of this long process, we see how the fruits of both the work's production and writing itself have ripened into an exceptional volume. The aptly and comically titled *The Antediluvian Librarians' Secrets for Success* will be a most welcome addition to this genre of "writing help" books. It is also of importance for us here at Bridwell, because it has been undertaken by highly trained and experienced staff, who have long been in the trenches of theological writing, training, and stewardship. What this work does, and how it differs from any other works, is that it provides a thoughtful, intuitive, and empathic approach to theological writing. In many ways it is a palliative grammar of the writing soul, a primer on how to prepare your approach to both writing and the seminary experience. This pedagogy is long overdue, but will be most appreciated by its users. The lexical content is complemented graciously by the magnificent art of Rebecca Howdeshell, which is abstract and linear in form, while aesthetically provocative and stimulating. The choice of this combination will surely mark this volume as significant and the work itself will stand out as an important addition to the canon of books on writing practice. *The Antediluvian Librarians' Secrets for Success* is also the first publication in our new professional publications initiative at Bridwell Library—*Bridwell Press*. The goal of our press is to publish works as freely accessible e-books for greater reach and accessibility with print-on-demand options. Our history as a place of content creation and publishing is significant—the library itself has published more than 100 titles in 70 years—and continues to provide a space for high quality research and writing. With this new model we believe that publishing will also be more central to the work that we do. And with this present volume, we launch *Bridwell Press* and invite you into our global community of research, writing, and publishing.

Finally, we are proud of our colleagues and those who have brought this to fruition and happy to share this new work with all of you. We hope you enjoy and find it most rewarding and helpful in your journey toward better writing. As Kafka actually said: "All human errors are impatience…," so we must take time, be deliberate, and pay attention to the wisdom of this excellent volume.

Anthony J. Elia
Director and J.S. Bridwell Foundation Endowed Librarian
Bridwell Library

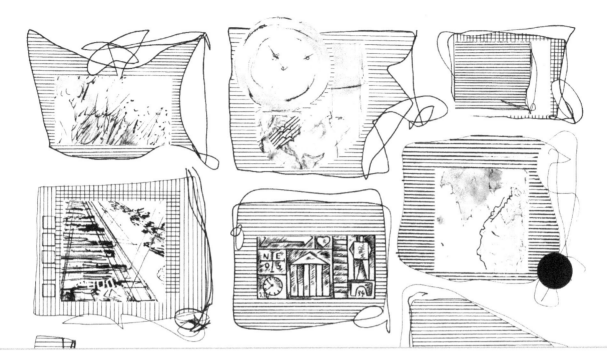

PART ONE: BEFORE YOU BEGIN, ORIENT YOURSELF

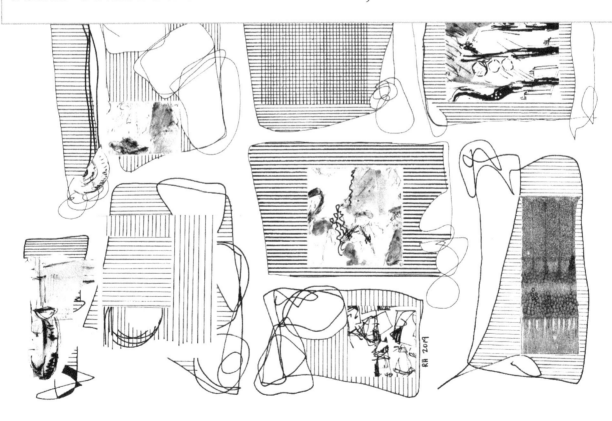

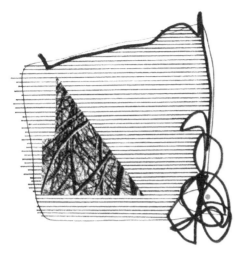

Ask for Help and You Shall Receive It

Starting a graduate program is confusing, and you will confront many things you do not know. Do not be afraid to ask for help, and remember: you belong here!

So here you are at the beginning of your graduate career, overwhelmed by unfamiliar faces, geography, vocabulary, and tasks. You wonder if you accidentally missed an essential meeting in which all institutional wisdom was revealed, because everyone else in your incoming class seems to already know about this stuff. The Antediluvian Librarians feel safe in saying you should not let the assurance of your classmates worry you; we're pretty certain they're bluffing.

The Antediluvian Librarians also feel secure in asserting that nobody likes to say "I don't know." It makes us feel uncomfortable and vulnerable, and many of us believe that it makes a bad impression. Yet until we admit that we don't know something, we are unlikely to get to a place where we can learn about it. Don't fixate on the fact that you don't know something. Instead, use your time and energy to find out about it. This practice will yield two positive results. First, you will know one more thing and, second, you will get that boost in confidence that comes from doing something courageous. Think about it. You didn't know, but you admitted it and got help in finding out—one of the bravest things anyone can do. Then if you get into the practice of asking questions like "How can I learn more about this?" whenever something unfamiliar comes along, you will have created an important habit, as well as rapidly growing in both knowledge and confidence. Who's bluffing now?

The process is as simple as getting yourself a notebook and keeping it handy. Whenever something perplexes you, write it down and pledge to solve the mystery. You have far more resources at your disposal than you imagine. It could be campus geography. *Which way is north?* It could be coping with day-to-day life. *What color is my assigned parking lot?* It could even be Theology. *What do you mean there are two St. Augustines?* There is a library full of books and a school full of people, all of whom vividly recall their first few weeks in a new program. Remember that all of us have started where you are right now, and we are eager to help.

Rest assured that demystification is available all around you. If you ask for help, you shall receive it. Usually over lunch!

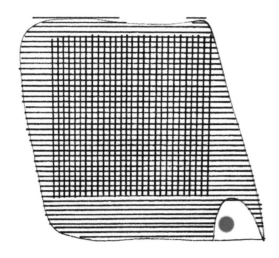

Graduate School Differs from What You've Done Before

Graduate school involves different expectations from college or your career, so you need to prepare for it. Help is always available through institutional resources (like advisors and librarians) and personal connections.

Many people assume that graduate or graduate professional school is like an extension of college, but the experiences of graduate students vary from those of undergraduates in significant ways. Therefore, to avoid unpleasant shocks and unnecessary frustration, it is best to adjust your expectations accordingly.

One essential distinction, of course, is that everyone is here because they want to be. People go to college for a variety of reasons, but graduate students have chosen to enroll. Your professors are going to assume that you're interested in being here and that you're prepared to work at it. They will try to keep it engaging, but they will expect you to hold up your end by coming to class prepared to study and participate intensively in the fields of theology, biblical studies, church history, pastoral care, Christian education, or sacred music. Your professors may expect you to develop new knowledge in that field through research or by applying specialized knowledge to real world situations. That being said, you can check your beginning-of-the-semester jitters at the door. You won't be asked to undertake any of these tasks unprepared. Know that you can do this; you would not have been admitted otherwise.

The Antediluvian Librarians often hear statements like, "I can't do that—I was an accounting major." Or, "I've been a nurse for thirty years, I have never written a history paper." Or, "Everybody seems to have a Religious Studies background except me." The diversity of the student body of any seminary or theology school is its greatest strength. God calls people from all walks of life, at all times of life, with every sort of educational and career background or social and cultural contexts. If you feel under-prepared for an assignment, simply talk to your professor, your TA, your librarians, or your advisor. Work with a writing center, a study group, or a student organization. And look to your classmates.

Your classmates are your future professional colleagues, many of whom will live out their careers with you, whether you continue in the church, the academy, or somewhere altogether else. They know what drives you, frustrates you, or fills you with joy, because they are going through it with you. The people you meet in school are possibly the greatest resource you'll have in your profession. In the meantime, they are one of the best resources you'll have throughout your studies. If you don't understand something, chances are that many of your classmates don't understand it either. After all, faculty have off days, too, and maybe that whole transubstantiation lecture was presented at a time when Professor Broody was enduring an extended visit from a disagreeable mother-in-law.

In Praise of Stupid Questions

There are no stupid questions, we promise. Please ask when you feel like you are stuck in the dark.

We have all heard it said, "There are no stupid questions." The Antediluvian Librarians strongly endorse the sentiment behind that statement. While there may be questions phrased in ways that are less elegant than they might be—thereby coming close to the category of stupid—the curiosity and need that prompts them is **never** stupid. To put it more specifically, as astrophysicist Carl Sagan said, "There are naïve questions, tedious questions, ill-phrased questions, questions put after inadequate self-criticism. But every question is a cry to understand the world. There is no such thing as a dumb question."

Questions are the lifeblood of academic life. They indicate people's curiosity, analytical abilities, and desire to learn. Asking questions is hard, but well worth it in the end. No one knows that better than those who teach because they have to ask hundreds of questions to help their students learn. Questions open doors to understanding. A seemingly naïve question can cast new light on old assumptions. Further, if you have questions, it's a sure bet that your classmates do too. They just may be afraid to speak up. Remember the emperor and his new clothes?

So, ask questions—lots and lots of questions.
Even if you worry the answer may be obvious.
Even if you fear they are unsophisticated.
Even if you aren't sure about the vocabulary.
Even if you suspect your professor will become impatient.
Even if you think your fellow students may laugh.
Even if . . .
Even.

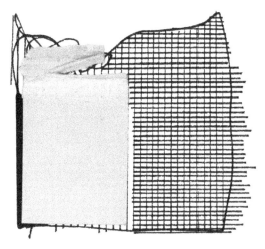

Know Thyself

A good understanding of your own weaknesses and strengths can help immensely as you prepare to enter Theology School.

Personal formation is an essential aspect of theological education. In the end, the goal of seminary (and of education) is less about filling our heads with knowledge than it is forming the habit of learning and transforming the character of those who learn. Theology school is not only intellectually challenging, but also brings us face to face with profound, life-changing questions about God, the universe, and ourselves. Perhaps this is why the words "know thyself" (ΓΝΩΘΙ ΣΕΑΥΤΟΝ) were carved above the entrance to the oracle at Delphi: encountering sublime mysteries compels us to take stock of our abilities and shortcomings, our strengths and our weaknesses. Such self-awareness requires honesty, humility, and courage.

The Antediluvian Librarians feel safe in asserting that nobody wants to dwell on the things they can't do well; we all prefer playing to our strengths. Yet ignoring a weakness, especially in church or academic life, can lead to unsatisfactory consequences. Where would we be if Thomas Aquinas had found philosophy too challenging? Or if Saint Cecelia believed it when her kindergarten teacher said she couldn't carry a tune? It took Augustine years before he could exercise restraint, but look at his accomplishments once he did.

Rather than beating ourselves up—or worse, ignoring our weaknesses in hopes that they will go away—we need to suck it up and face them. If we can honestly assess the areas that give us trouble, then invest our best efforts in bringing them up to an adequate standard, we win by improving both our habits and self-awareness. Let's not kid ourselves, however. Sincere personal assessment takes humility and perseverance. It runs counter to our culture and our own natures, but it's well worth it in the long term—the communion of saints tells us so.

Once we are over that hurdle, it becomes a matter of classifying the problem and seeking a remedy. Is the problem area knowledge-based? This category includes skills like accounting, a strong vocabulary, or coping with the latest technology—all things that anyone can objectively learn and practice. Perhaps it is more in the area of administrative skills, like problem solving, managing people, or communications? These skills are trickier because they are subjective, but seeking guidance from more experienced people, plus plain old trial and error, should help. Maybe it hits closer to home in the area of personal traits, like punctuality, optimism, or assertiveness? The fix here could be as simple as buying an alarm clock or as tough as seeking professional guidance. Or there are the skills one can acquire only through doing them, over and over, like public speaking, writing well, or riding a bicycle.

And while we are getting to know ourselves, we need to take inventory of our strengths. Knowing what comes easily for us, and developing habits that play to our strengths, is a hallmark of working smarter. Just like taking an inventory of our weaknesses, figuring out our strengths involves self-examination. It's highly personal, but it can yield many positive results. For example, if you know you have a facility for languages, that should play a part in your selection of courses in Theology School. If you possess a talent for pastoral care, that should, too. If history is your great love, then you should consider concentrating on classes in Christian Heritage.

Finally, to take self-knowledge a step further, the Antediluvian Librarians invite you to examine the specific factors that motivate you to learn deeply and well. For some people it is the idea of being of service to others. Some perceive what they have to learn as having a long-term benefit for their lives and careers. In many ways, you have probably already connected the idea of seminary work with your personal goals and professional priorities. Create a list of distinct personal motivating factors, and connect them with your inventory of weaknesses and strengths. What you will have created is not only a road map of where and how you should invest your time and energy, but also a safety net for those times when, inevitably, you find yourself asking, "What am I doing here?" Trust us. We've been there.

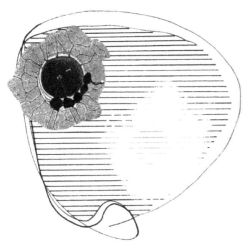

And Know a Few Other Things, Too

Taking even more time to familiarize yourself with various aspects of the new world you are about to enter allows you to maximize your time later in the semester, make informed decisions about what direction you want your graduate career to take, and can ease the transition to life as a student.

The Antediluvian Librarians feel strongly that there are three more things with which we should be familiar as we cross the threshold into graduate work in theology: commonly used software, the members of your faculty, and the language of theology.

These topics are a motley assortment, granted. Yet, each can have profound practical implications for your success in class. So, as just one example, if you are not adept at using one of the standard word processing programs, now is the time to learn it. You will be spending countless hours taking notes and writing papers in the years ahead. Knowing your options for formatting, inserting charts, graphs, and images, and appending reference notes will save you a lot of grief when deadlines loom. Check to see if your new institution offers various software packages either for free or for sale at a discounted student price, then go online to find videos that teach you how to use it. The same applies to your new institution's Learning Management Software, like Blackboard or Canvas; online conferencing tools, like Zoom or Skype; presentation software like PowerPoint or Prezi; and even Bible software, like Accordance.

Just as crucial as learning basic software is gaining a sense of the members of your new faculty. If one professor were the same as another, there'd be no need for RateMyProfessors.com. While we understand that many factors play into a student's decision to take a class, including when, where, and how it is offered or whether it fulfills a requirement, more important still is the question of WHO is teaching the class. Over and above making an effort to learn the names and faces of the faculty, reviewing you school's faculty biographies is a must. You will learn who covers the fields of study that interest you the most, what they have published and how recently, and what their perspective is. Remember that your theological education should challenge your assumptions and make you think more deeply about them. For example, you shouldn't necessarily avoid taking a class with someone whose views do not completely agree with your own. Such a class may present you with a splendid opportunity to stretch yourself.

Finally, the new world of theology has its own language. Nobody expects you to speak this language from Day One, but a good dictionary of theological terms will serve you just as well as a language phrase book on a trip overseas. There are a wide variety of such dictionaries available; used paperbacks can be had for a few dollars, and they will save you from looking blank if you are encountering the word "hermeneutics" for the very first time. Your school's library will have the more comprehensive (and expensive) dictionaries available either online or in their reference room. These may include *The Westminster Dictionary of Theological Terms* as well as the various lexicons of theological terms in Latin, Greek, and modern European languages. But for the purposes of getting by in your first few weeks, a modest paperback will serve you well.

Books We Wish We Had Read before Coming to Seminary or Theology School

The Bible, preferably in a study version with notes and commentary.

Adler, Mortimer J. and Carl Van Doren. *How to Read a Book: The Classic Guide to Intelligent Reading.* New York: Touchstone, revised edition, 1972.

Cooper, Stephen A. *Augustine for Armchair Theologians.* Louisville, KY: Westminster John Knox Press, 2002.

Core, Deborah. *The Seminary Student Writes.* Saint Louis, MO: Chalice Press, 2000.

Frankl, Viktor E. *Man's Search for Meaning.* Boston: Beacon Press, 2006.

Gaarder, Jostein. *Sophie's World: A Novel About the History of Philosophy.* New York: Farrar, Straus and Girous, 1994.

González, Justo L. *The Story of Christianity.* San Francisco: Harper & Row, 1984.

Harris, Roberta L. *The World of the Bible.* New York: Thames and Hudson, 1995.

King, Martin Luther. *Strength to Love.* New York: Harper & Row, 1963.

Lewis, C. S. *Mere Christianity.* San Francisco: HarperOne, 2015.

Moore, Christopher. *Lamb: The Gospel According to Biff, Christ's Childhood Pal.* New York: Perennial, 2003.

Palmer, Parker. *Let Your Life Speak: Listening for the Voice of Vocation.* San Francisco: Jossey-Bass, 2000.

Stone, Howard W. and James O. Duke. *How to Think Theologically.* Minneapolis, MN: Fortress Press 2013.

Wink, Walter. *The Powers That Be: Theology for a New Millennium.* New York: Doubleday, 1998.

PART TWO: ONCE YOU HAVE BEGUN

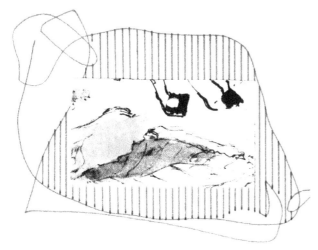

Think Before You Buy

Before you rush out to spend significant sums of money on the latest whatever, think carefully about the investment of that other valuable asset: your time.

One of the sad facts of life is that a Stradivarius does not make a better violinist, nor a Porsche a better driver. Elite equipment requires elite skills and can sometimes cause those who are not ready for it to perform more poorly than they would with more appropriate choices. The goal is to have equipment that is suitable for one's skill level, needs, and potential for growth. It takes time, discipline, and dedication to develop expertise—like learning to use an Apple computer if deep down inside you're really a PC person.

Of course, we can aspire to elite tools, but we should never expect the tools to do the job on our behalf. Tools are simply tools, not magical talismans that imbue us with an indefinable glamour just by being seen using them. Nor can tools complete your tasks for you—Snow White may have had the help of singing woodland creatures, but she still wielded the mop herself. Nevertheless, marketers often make impossible claims for the products they want to sell us, and that applies to academic products, too. Think about your needs as well as your goals before opening your wallet.

Some expensive snares for theology students can include pricey Bible software packed with hundreds of different versions of the text with apparatus to tracking every word in forty or more languages. Such a database may not be the best place to start the journey to becoming a better exegete and preacher. All those whiz-bang options can mislead and overwhelm you if you don't understand the fundamentals of exegesis. Learn to do exegesis step-by-step with a discounted student version of the same product, or even the tried-and-true print resources at your library. That way you can develop a foundation in biblical criticism and decide if that is where your future might lie before parting with several hundred dollars.

By the same token, a computer has yet to be designed that can improve your writing for you. A word processor may help you write more efficiently, but it won't enhance your paper's quality. And if you believe you can rely on tools like spell check to catch errors, just read a bit further; this volume includes a list of our favorite spell check oversights. The bottom line is that we are all better off simply choosing hardware and software that we are comfortable working with rather than what the tech geeks, or our children, think is cool. That way, we can actually get down to the business of writing. A lot. All the time. Which is actually the only way one's writing will improve.

Finally, if you are in the market for any kind of specialized software, be sure to explore what your institution has to offer. Or at the very least, what its IT department will support. Investigate what is available for free, like shareware programs, and look at their longevity. Many reputable options exist for all sorts of academic purposes. And of course, it pays to familiarize yourself with your institutional library—the best free resource of them all.

Time Management

The beginning of a bright, shiny new term is exactly the right time to get proactive. Grab your syllabi and your calendar and invest the time to plan out your semester.

Many of us know that effective scheduling is a key factor for success in any area of life. When we have command of our schedules—the deadlines, meetings, due dates, etc.—life runs far more smoothly because we have minimized the chances for ugly surprises.

There are several ways to maintain control of our commitments, from the old reliable paper calendar to the latest app for smart phones. Regardless of the method you choose, here are some good habits to consider adopting:

1. Keep *one single calendar*. There is an old aphorism about a person with one clock knowing what time it is, while the person with two is never quite sure. Trying to maintain multiple calendars simply leads to confusion and, inevitably, there will always be something that doesn't make the transfer from one to the other.

2. Commit to reading through all your course syllabi *carefully*. Make notes of any questions you have (if you have them, your classmates will, too) and enter every deadline, reading assignment, and other time-sensitive item into your calendar. For large deadlines, enter warnings for yourself a few days, or even weeks, earlier. Include any other important dates in your life: Thanksgiving, Spring Break, your anniversary, your mom's birthday, etc.

3. Schedule time for problem solving. Snags and detours are a part of life. Build in time to address the problems you will encounter from time to time. Knowing you have the space to deal with them will also help reduce the stress that these problems bring with them.

If managing your time remains a challenge, there's always an answer online: time management charts, apps, and other resources are readily available. The key to any of them, however, is that you use them. They are only as good as your determination to keep them up to date. Consider it your personal commitment to stress management and self-care, because in the end, that is what good time management amounts to.

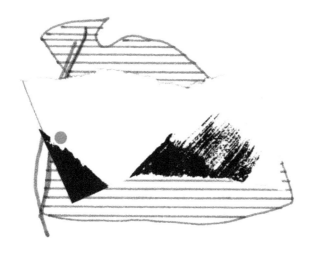

Reading Strategically

There is more than one way to skin a cat, and there is more than one way to read a book. Active reading is the goal toward which you should strive.

The Episcopal *Book of Common Prayer* encourages us to "read, mark, learn, and inwardly digest." This is also excellent advice for seminary. These four elements are the essential components of reading for school, in contrast to reading for pleasure—the four elements of which should be sun, sand, water, and a cocktail waiter. Here are some practices that may help you now and for upcoming exams.

Reading: Reading does not mean picking up material, starting at the beginning, going through to the end, and putting it down. Instead try some of these ideas: survey the information that tells you what the piece is about, including abstracts (brief summaries of articles), introductions, reviews, dust jackets, tables of content, section headings, illustration captions, etc. Read introductions to learn about the work as a whole and for its components, then scan the major sections before plunging in. Introductions help you get the gist of a piece; you don't necessarily have to read every word of the whole thing. If, however, the information is particularly cogent to a class or project, then plan to read it closely.

Marking: To use a highlighter while reading is to passively engage with material. To outline and summarize is to have control of it. Make notes of your reading as you go along and stop every so often to encapsulate an author's points. Copy out direct quotations that strike you as especially significant. Engaging in these ways makes the material part of you, almost like an education!

Learning: Make it a point to teach yourself the bits and pieces of your reading that you do not understand. This is easily accomplished with a regular dictionary, a subject-specific dictionary, or some of your textbooks (but ***not*** Wikipedia). You are aiming for absolute clarity on a subject, and obscure vocabulary or concepts prevent you from achieving that. Question those things that confuse you. There's a good chance that they are confusing the rest of your classmates as well.

Inwardly digesting: Go through your notes before class and edit them during classroom discussion. Review them again after class—the same day if possible. Ask yourself how the reading connects with the lectures and make a few notes on that as well. Small investments of time throughout the semester can result in huge rewards when you get to test time.

Other methods for actively engaging with a piece of writing can include questioning the writer. Think about why she went to the trouble of writing this piece and then ask yourself why you should go to the trouble of reading it. What is at stake, for the author and for yourself?

Whether you agree with what the writer is saying or not, don't accept her assertions at face value. What are the writer's biases? Her social location or historical context? Are the arguments and evidence relevant and presented clearly? Do they support the writer's conclusions? Are there other issues that occur to you that the author has not addressed? Be skeptical. Consider your own context. Are you left with any questions?

Finally consider these things as you read:

- What is the work's genre and intended audience?

- Is it exploring a particular position or is it a broad survey of a topic?

- Why do you think your professor assigned it? It might be to deliberately provoke you rather than simply to impart information.

- How does this reading connect with class lectures and discussions?

- Does this reading have implications or usefulness for classes other than the one for which it was assigned?

- When was this work written and in what cultural/historical context? This is particularly important for texts more than 50 years old, whether primary or secondary sources.

Effective Note-Taking

Unfortunately, there are no shortcuts to learning. There are, however, efficiencies. Efficient and effective note-taking are perhaps the best investments of your time that you can make.

Sometimes taking notes in graduate school gets intense. A lot of information is thrown at us, and if we aren't prepared to catch it, we miss it. The trick is to get organized (a whole 'nother topic) and to keep note-taking simple, because when you review your notes, you'll want a summary, **not a transcription**.

Taking notes is also personal, idiosyncratic, and determined by whatever format works best for you, whether you are writing on paper or entering information into a word document, a personally designed table, or a bibliographic software program. Any system you are comfortable using consistently will do. What follows are a few ways to improve whatever system you are using already.

First, think in terms of keeping your notes succinct, focusing especially on key words and concepts that will trigger your memory of lectures and readings. The fundamental factor in achieving good notes is to fully engage the gears of your brain while you read or listen to a lecture. Contrary to what you may have observed, you cannot read or listen effectively while browsing social media, so Step One is to pay attention. As you read/listen, determine what information is truly relevant. Look for key concepts, themes, and terms.

Your course syllabus will provide clues to concepts and patterns; after all, your professors have painstakingly thought up and typed out the goals and themes for the course. Ask yourself how the information you are hearing or reading fits into the direction and emphasis your professor has in mind. Active, analytical listening such as this will help you retain the information flying past you. Another clue is that writers and lecturers use repetition for emphasis; anything worth saying is worth saying twice.

As mentioned above, you can't, and shouldn't, write down everything being said. Summarization on the fly is hard, but it gets easier with practice. Further, it not only keeps your notes manageable, it also quickly reveals which points you understand and which you do not. Translating the subject matter into your own words becomes remarkably difficult when the concepts are murky. When a point made in class puzzles you, continue to take notes as best you can but put a big circle around it to remind yourself to seek clarification later. Always make a point to review your notes soon after class—

preferably the same day—so errors can be corrected and remaining questions identified. Even if you have only a few minutes, this kind of review while the lecture is fresh in your memory is better than hours of wracking your brain at a much later date.

Another part of taking good notes in class is getting to know the professor. While you are learning her style and idiosyncrasies, tune into the following clues that can serve to highlight information she considers important:

- Changes of pace, like slowing down so you can get it all, or using more volume/emphasis;

- Class handouts or anything in the syllabus that is starred, bolded, or highlighted;

- Anything written on the board or included in a PowerPoint—which is why God includes cameras in our phones;

- Anything preceded by "first, then," or "First, second, and finally," etc. This is the verbal form of outlining;

- Anything that implies a relationship between topics: "on one hand," "on the other hand," or "on the third hand";

- Anything that suggests that the topic stands in contrast to another topic, or that one derives from the other;

- Language that indicates the topic is a "hot-button" issue in the academy or in everyday life.

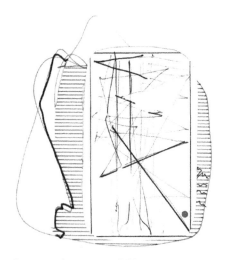

Critical Thinking and Critical Humility

Theological education is all about thinking critically but non-judgmentally, seeing the world from multiple perspectives, and letting go of self-interest for a more charitable view of others.

Just as there are different ways to read, there are different ways to think. In graduate school you may hear people refer to critical thinking skills, which can be an umbrella term for several ways of thinking that stand us in good stead as we pursue theological education. They include the ability to think in the abstract and concrete, to think imaginatively and creatively, to think analytically and logically, etc. In common parlance, these methods of thinking encompass things like problem solving, "thinking outside the box," "putting yourself in someone else's shoes," philosophizing, deducing (like Sherlock Holmes), decision-making, and many others.

The image that appeals to the Antediluvian Librarians comes from an old movie called "The Man Who Would Be King" (1975), in which a pair of adventurers played by Michael Caine and Sean Connery stumble upon a treasure room filled with huge gemstones. Michael Caine holds up a ruby the size of a grapefruit and turns it in his hand to see all its many facets. Critical thinking is like looking at all the different facets of a ruby, trying to understand a single object or idea by viewing it from many different angles.

The angles with which we view an idea or an object constitute perspective. We each have our own perspective, which is often called our social location. Social location is determined by our time, place, and personal circumstances. One's social location and perspective can easily become contentious in these troubled times, and that's where Critical Humility comes into play. Critical Humility is the antithesis of being judgmental; it's a willingness to set aside your own vested interests in order to find out about someone else's views, experiences, perspectives. As Christians, we are urged to walk humbly. Taking it a step further, perhaps we should also "think humbly." Thinking humbly opens us up to the process of learning—in class and in society. It is acknowledging not only our own perspective, but those of our neighbors—both past and present. Its hallmark is refraining from arrogant assumptions and uncharitable judgments, as well as maintaining the awareness that the opinions and circumstances of others may be far different from our own (yet still valid). This applies both to the present and to the past.

Critical humility is especially necessary when thinking about history. It's easy to fall into the trap of thinking people in previous millennia were simply wrongheaded, unenlightened, stupid, or bigoted. Hindsight being 20/20, it is easy to judge the people of other centuries by the standards of today. This is called Presentism, i.e. the uncritical embrace of present-day attitudes, and the interpretation of the past in terms of modern values and concepts. Our present perspective offers many insights into societies distant from us in time and space, but we need to be charitable about them as well. We should remember that in twenty-first century America more people have much more personal freedom and many more fundamental rights than people on other continents and in other ages. For example, think about the clothes you are wearing right now. Did you know that in the past even the colors and styles of clothing people wore were often regulated by sumptuary laws designed to reinforce the rank and privilege one enjoyed—or did not—in society? So rather than rail against Thomas Aquinas's attitude toward women, look at his work as a reflection of the position held by women in 13th century Italian society. Of course, you should call attention to the sins of omission and commission in the work of past theologians, but also grant them the respect they deserve for working to the best of their abilities given their time and place. After all, they are only human.

As the above illustration demonstrates, critical humility applies to both the people we encounter, and the texts we engage with. It means allowing texts to speak with their own voice, from their own time and place. It is humble, in that we acknowledge that there are things we do not know, and that the text has something to teach us. It is critical in that we posit challenging questions to the text, such as "why does the author say that here?" Perhaps nowhere is this stance more important than when we are reading sacred texts with their power to transform lives, or harm if wrongly used. Searching the scriptures means not only engaging them with intellectual rigor, but also being open to hearing the truth they convey.

Resources for Once You Have Begun

Gawande, Atul. *The Checklist Manifesto: How to Get Things Right.* New York: Metropolitan Books, 2010.

Haber, Jonathan. "It's Time to Get Serious about Teaching Critical Thinking." *Inside Higher Education* (March 2, 2020): https://www.insidehighered.com/views/2020/03/02/teaching-students-think-critically-opinion

"How to Read Like a Grad Student." *History in High Heels* [blog], October 13, 2013: http://historyinhighheels.com/2013/10/how-to-read-like-a-grad-student/

Kahneman, Daniel. *Thinking, Fast and Slow.* New York: Farrar, Straus and Giroux, 2011.

Nhât Hanh, and Mai Vo-Dinh. *The Miracle of Mindfulness: A Manual on Meditation.* Boston: Beacon Press, 1987.

Rampton, John. "Manipulate Time with These Powerful 20 Time Management Tips." *Forbes* (May 1, 2018): https://www.forbes.com/sites/johnrampton/2018/05/01/manipulate-time-with-these-powerful-20-time-management-tips/#403ead857ab4

"Taking Notes while Reading." The Learning Center, University of North Carolina at Chapel Hill. https://learningcenter.unc.edu/tips-and-tools/taking-notes-while-reading/

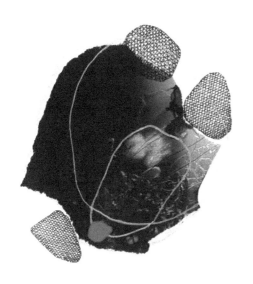

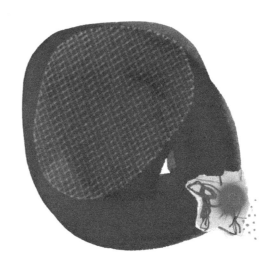

PART THREE: HABITS TO LAST A LIFETIME

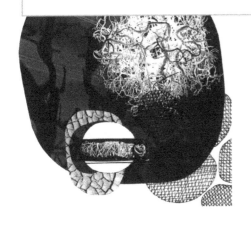

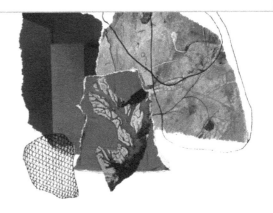

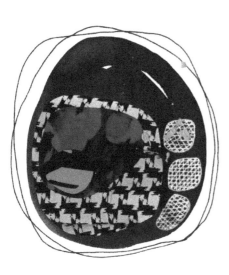

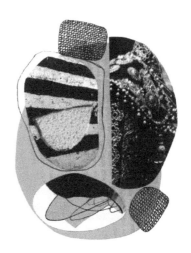

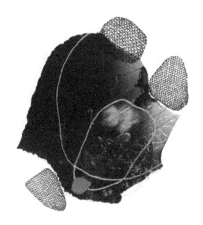

The Myth of Multitasking

Starting a graduate program is confusing and feeling completely at sea is normal. You will confront many things you do not know. Do not be afraid to ask for help.

We all multi-task out of necessity; it's the world we live in. While it is too easy to get swept up in the hustle of academic life, church life, family life, etc., perhaps the best opportunity we have to cultivate inner calm and intentionality is in the midst of such chaos. As a student you have the responsibility of creating space for yourself so that you can listen, study, reflect, and write. Theology is a serious task that requires your undivided attention. Self-awareness is key. If you look at the lives of the desert fathers and think, "Wow, a cave in the wilderness free from distractions sounds really good right now," then you might want to take a closer look at where and how you are investing your energy.

Begin by considering when it might be OK to multitask. Do you listen to audio files of class lectures or readings while you do household chores or exercise? Well done. That is an excellent way to maximize your time. Have you ever checked your cell phone (more than once, anyway) while meeting with a member of your congregation or your bishop? Nope. Such a gesture in a private meeting is unlikely to end well for you. These are clear-cut, black and white examples. What you need to decide for yourself is how to handle the fuzzy gray areas in between.

Imagine yourself in some real-life situations and decide how you will handle them now, when you are detached and thinking clearly. Can or should you multitask while:

- Stuck in gridlock traffic?

- Speeding down the highway at 70 MPH?

- Riding on public transportation?

- Sharing a meal with buddies?

- Sharing a meal with the church council?

- Listening to your professor lecture?

- Trying to study or write?

Of course, the answer to some of these questions is conditional, depending on context and urgency. For example, if you are in a class and look something up in the online *Oxford Dictionary of the Christian Church* to contribute to the discussion, that would be fine. Sitting in class messing around on Instagram or checking scores during the MLB playoff (as at least one of the Antediluvian Librarians was caught doing), is perhaps more questionable. If you know you need to unplug, yet you have responsibilities like a sick child or a parishioner who is in the hospital, you might consider giving your phone to a trusted friend so that they can monitor your messages and interrupt in case of emergency. This allows you to be connected, but not distracted, either by the phone or by worrying about not knowing who or what you might be missing.

The bottom line is to be aware of when you are dividing your attention and make conscious choices to focus on the task at hand. It is a life skill worth cultivating. If you're having trouble completing your class reading, perhaps silencing your cell phone for a couple of hours is a reasonable tradeoff. Develop the awareness of when multitasking will have a negative impact and develop strategies to prevent the problem based on your personal priorities and values. The world will not cease to exist if you take a moment to step back and consider where and how to direct your focus.

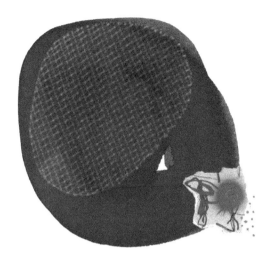

Take Good Care of Yourself

Self-care is essential for a successful career in theology school, and even more so afterwards. Consider adopting these practices to keep yourself at peak performance.

Graduate work in theology is a marathon, not a sprint. To make it to the finish line you must be in good condition, and cultivate habits of self-care. Treating yourself well is not an act of selfishness, because you can't do other people any good if you are in bad shape yourself. Look upon your own wellbeing as you would that of your child, or your pets, or a beloved car, and give yourself the attention you deserve.

Get Enough Sleep. If you are over 30, those all-nighters you remember from your undergraduate career are tougher and tougher to pull off without serious repercussions. A normal bedtime will do you more good than the extra hours of cramming for an exam. If you are feeling short on sleep and need to catch up, try going to bed earlier rather than sleeping later.

Eat Properly. If you are an anxious eater, you will seek out all sorts of junk foods in times of heightened stress. Rather than deprive yourself of the ice cream or chips, try to defer eating them until after you've had a healthy meal. By waiting until you are already full you are less likely to binge, yet you can still satisfy that nagging crave. Also try not to eat heavily before bedtime, which can interfere with sleep.

Exercise. There's no need to become a tri-athlete; a twenty-minute stroll across campus will work just fine. See if you can incorporate small bits of exertion into your daily routine: climbing stairs, parking further out, bench-pressing your week's reading assignments. It's easier, and more effective, to maintain such little habits on a regular basis than to sporadically try to adopt a more time-consuming regimen.

Relax. Punctuate your day with breaks to help keep your mind fresh and focused. Every half hour take 60 seconds to close your eyes, sit still, and do some deep breathing. Or praying. Every hour walk around for five minutes, but not to the fridge or the pantry. At the end of the day take some time to clear your head and wind down so your sleep will be more restful. Sitting outside, soaking in a warm tub, or fixing yourself a warm drink are effective options.

Seek Social Support. It's kind of what theology schools do, right? You are surrounded by colleagues, pals, and faculty who have all been where you are. If you begin to feel panicky, sit down with one of them for a chat. Talking things over with someone who knows the score can give you the boost you need.

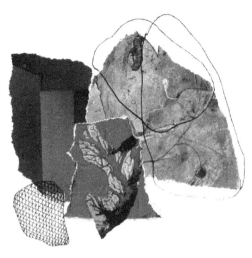

Cordial Discourse

Discourse: *The verbal interchange of ideas. Not to be confused with "discord."*

Cordial: *Warmly and genially affable, see gracious.*

Controversy, contention, and unsolicited opinions surround us, especially in election years. As theological students who may soon lead churches and other organizations, we must learn the art of cordial conversation so that we can conduct it ourselves and initiate it among others. Sadly, these days respectful communication is the exception rather than the rule. How many times have you come away from a personal conversation, a social media chat, or even a classroom discussion feeling bruised because someone confused debate with denigration? Or mistook provoking thought with provoking anger? Or dominated the conversation out of all proportion to the number of people trying to participate?

Cordial dialogue is challenging when examining controversial issues, especially when we have a deep commitment to our own positions. It is essential to care for our own identities yet simultaneously refrain from disparaging the identity and beliefs of the people whose positions differ from ours. To help maintain this tricky balance we must try our best to distinguish between the person for whom we should care and their ideas, which may not be entirely to our taste. The very nature of theological education is to engage in discussion of charged topics in order to grow in knowledge and understanding. Theology students in the United States sometimes forget what a rare gift they enjoy. Any number of people around the globe envy our ability to engage in free and open debate. Rather than abuse our colleagues, we should remember those less fortunate, cherish our privilege, and cultivate good conversational habits.

The elements that make for a productive exchange of ideas include respect, receptivity, and a firm grasp of increasingly un-common courtesy. Honesty is a virtue as long as participants are employing it in a constructive way; too often, though, bullies use it as an excuse for bludgeoning people. Regardless of the mix of participants, here are a few guidelines to bear in mind in both your own conversations and when you engage in, or lead, group discussions:

- Remember that the goal of most discourse is to air and understand diverse ideas rather than to "win."

- Give every member of the group ample opportunity to speak freely and voice their concerns.

- Foster an atmosphere of give and take, even for ideas that are not fully formed. You should create an environment in which people feel safe speaking.

- Calmly and politely squash anyone's attempt to dominate, interrupt, or intimidate.

- Encourage respectful and constructive feedback. Discourage negativity.

- Be ruthless in shutting down any line of conversation that threatens to violate rules of common courtesy.

- Remind everyone that they share a common goal and are playing for the same team.

- Keep your own cool, too.

- If necessary, remove toxic people from the mix. If that is not possible, then have a word with them privately.

Remember that before you can agree or disagree with someone, you must first understand what they are saying. If the topic is too controversial for you to digest all at once, you can always opt to suspend judgment by saying, "I'd like to think about this and talk again." Social media has deluded us into thinking that we must respond immediately; don't fall into that trap. Take your time. Think about it. Give emotions time to subside. A joke once made the rounds that went something like this: "A priest, a rabbi, and an imam walked into a Starbucks. They had coffee and a calm conversation, because none of them were jerks." This is a useful image to bear in mind when you hear conversations degenerate into name-calling. After all, we're civilized human beings, not presidential candidates.

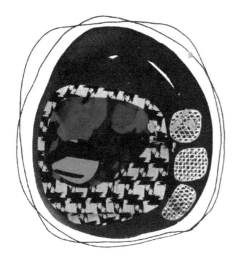

Comparisons Are Useless—You Do You

Don't fret if your classmates appear unfazed by the challenges of the first semester in theology school. They are bluffing. Deep down they are probably as rattled by their new circumstances as you are.

Theology is a unique field; it engages an educationally varied selection of people with a wealth of life experiences. Whether theological education represents your first, second, or even third career, rest assured that you possess unique competencies for success. Comparing yourself with anyone else you meet in school, however, can quickly undermine your confidence. Even the professors we admire so much and who seem so wise, knowledgeable, and confident will admit to feeling overwhelmed, panicked, and inadequate when faced with something new—such as having to abruptly take all their classes online in the spring of 2020.

As you begin your graduate career, it is essential for you to do you and avoid comparing yourself with your classmates. The whippersnapper with mad computer skills sitting next to you in Christian Heritage may never have had to speak persuasively in a boardroom setting. Your silver-haired classmate in Christian Ethics has wisdom and life experience but can no longer work through the night to pull a project together six hours before it's due. Terésa the nurse has never written an argument paper, and Samuel the community fundraiser has never taken a history course. Everyone around you has a different story and skill set. And like you, they, too, are learning to juggle the demands of small children, aging parents, spouses, church, jobs, school, commuting, etc. You each deserve a medal—and fourteen hours of uninterrupted sleep.

If you do find yourself wondering why everyone else seems to swim along effortlessly, please stop and think rather than give into a sense of panic. Panic only leads to resentment and poor choices. You are anxious because Joe is raving about his super-sophisticated Bible software, and Mary is all wrapped up in her bibliographic management utility. You feel like maybe you should look into these products, too. Just remember that it is equally likely that both Joe and Mary are looking at your system of taking notes, for example, or your undergraduate background in religious studies and feeling just as worried.

Before you rush out to download what your neighbors are using, or buy a new product, stop a minute to consider the cost to yourself—in terms of both money and time (an even more precious resource). If you are not good with technology, honestly assess if the effort of installing and learning Joe's software is worth it to you. Mary's bibliographic utility may be perfect for her because she is planning to pursue a doctorate. Are you? Of course not. Instead, what you need is the confidence to just do you.

Take stock of your strengths and weaknesses and plan your semester accordingly. Have you organized the parents' group at your child's school? Then you'll excel at coordinating group assignments. Have you ever purchased or refinanced a house? Then you have the determination to carry out a semester-long project. Can you jog every morning, work part-time, carry a full course-load, and talk with your long-distance sweetie late into the night? Your energy and enthusiasm will carry you over many rough patches. Not all of your colleagues will have these skills. Cherish them and stop worrying about the other guy.

Your first semester will be characterized by a sense of overload, punctuated by bouts of panic and occasional feelings of inadequacy. ***You are not alone***. Try to maintain a healthy perspective, ask for help when you need it, and take the time to look around and congratulate yourself on your successes thus far. Every. Single. One. They must be many, or you wouldn't be here in the first place.

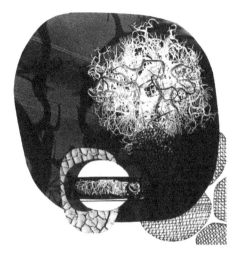

Giving and Receiving Criticism

Learning to think and speak analytically is an essential skill in theology school, but more important still is learning how to give and receive criticism graciously and constructively.

Criticism, also known as critical thinking or analytical thinking, is a crucial skill in an academic community, and the development of this skill is one of the primary goals of graduate education. Critiquing, in the academic sense, should always be constructive and delivered in a manner that is meant to promote clarity, understanding, and the common good. Contrary to some behaviors displayed in the media, criticism is not about winning or losing, and it is never about intentionally hurting an individual or group.

To deftly engage in responsible and productive criticism takes practice. For example, sarcasm may be funny in casual conversation, but in a serious discussion on a charged topic, it can be misconstrued and lead to anger and resentment. Here are some other guidelines to keep in mind during your next classroom discussion:

- If you feel like your statements have been misunderstood, remain calm and try to frame them differently.

- Be willing to admit that you don't know and haven't read everything. If you are unfamiliar with the sources on which people are basing their counter arguments, ask about them.

- If you are the recipient of harsh or unfair criticism, politely suggest that their statement might be rephrased in a less hurtful way. If that doesn't work, let it go and move on. Try not to nurse resentment.

- Focus your criticism on the idea, concept, or work under discussion rather than the person who created or delivered it.

  o Bad example: "The author Simon Scribbler is a racist homophobe, and Professor Tacitus should never have assigned his stupid book."

  o Good example: "The author Simon Scribbler's book reflects the unfortunate attitudes of his day and age, yet his analysis of the church in crisis during the Great Depression has valuable insights. Let's ask Professor Tacitus if that could be the reason she assigned it."

- Avoid labeling either the work or the person. Labels are often used dismissively.

    o Bad example: "As a disability theologian, of course you would say that."

    o Good example: "You know a lot about disability theology. Is that what's informing your views on this?"

- Ask questions rather than make statements:

    o Bad example: If you had read Miguel de la Torre, you'd see that your position could hardly apply to the global church.

    o Good example: Have you read Miguel de la Torre on this question? He has some interesting insights.

Resources for Habits to Last a Lifetime

Dickson, Charles. "How-to of Constructive Criticism." *The Priest* 64, no. 10 (October 2008): http://search.ebscohost.com.proxy.libraries.smu.edu/login.aspx?direct=true&db=lsdar&AN=CPLI0000470933&site=ehost-live&scope=site

Epperly, Bruce. *A Center in the Cyclone: Twenty-First Century Clergy Self Care.* Lanham, MD: Rowman & Littlefield, 2014.

Haas, Susan Biali. "How to Stop Comparing Yourself to Others." *Psychology Today* (March 5, 2018): https://www.psychologytoday.com/us/blog/prescriptions-life/201803/how-stop-comparing-yourself-others

Harrison Warren, Tish. "Meeting in the Middle: How the Concept of the via Media Might Help Restore Civil Discourse." *Christianity Today* 63, no. 9 (November 2019): 54–58. http://search.ebscohost.com.proxy.libraries.smu.edu/login.aspx?direct=true&db=lsdar&AN=ATLAiG0V191111000716&site=ehost-live&scope=site

Oliver, Pamela. "Taking Criticism While Privileged." *Inside Higher Ed* (July 18, 2018): https://www.insidehighered.com/advice/2018/07/18/advice-dealing-criticism-person-privilege-academe-opinion

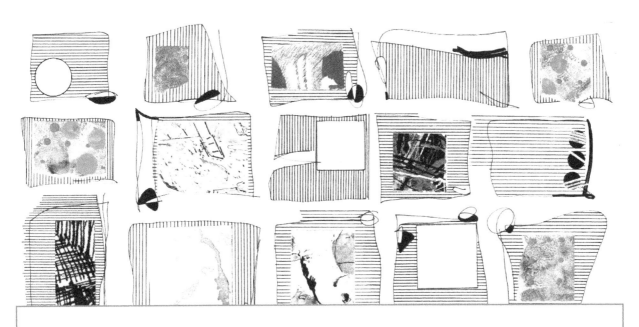

PART FOUR: THEOLOGICAL RESEARCH

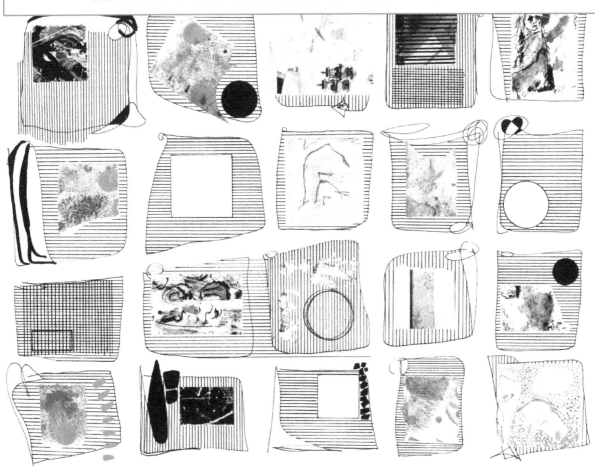

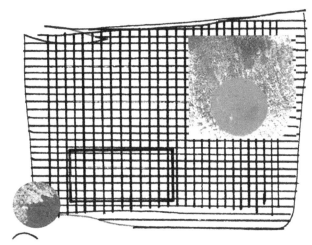

Resources to Know About

Use this quick guide to begin learning the best resources for your field—the ones you will rely on throughout your professional career.

With the number of resources—free and pricey, print and electronic—increasing every day, finding the right tool for your needs is a needle-in-a-haystack situation. Knowing where to look and knowing which tools are the best for which jobs will save time, energy, and frustration. For the fields of Theology and Religious Studies, we have rounded up our equivalents of hammer, screwdriver, pliers, and wrench, i.e. the top resources that anyone undertaking work in this area should know about. Just about every institution in the United States should provide access to these, either in print or online. We have included the basic reasons for their presence on this list as well.

- ATLA Religion Database. Outstanding for its depth, the ATLA Religion Database is *the* go-to database for research in religion and theology. It provides citations and full-text for scholarly articles, essays, and book reviews. Ignore it at your peril.

- ARDA: Association of Religion Data Archives. Search here for data, drawn from the Federal census, on churches and church membership, religious professionals and groups (individuals, congregations, and denominations), with interactive maps and statistics by state, county, and metropolitan area.

- Ministry Matters. A collection of commentaries, Bible dictionaries, and other reference works, including the *New Interpreter's Bible, New Interpreter's Dictionary of the Bible*, the Works of John Wesley, prayers and devotions, and various English versions of the Bible.

- Old Testament Abstracts and New Testament Abstracts. Provides abstracts (three- to four-sentence descriptions) for journal articles, monographs, multi-authored books, book reviews, and biblical software programs, capable of searching by specific scripture passage.

- Oxford Biblical Studies Online. Includes searchable texts such as the *New Oxford Annotated Bible*, and reference works such as the *Encyclopedia of the Dead Sea Scrolls*, *Oxford Bible Atlas*, and the *Oxford Companion to the Bible*.

- Oxford Bibliographies Online. Broken down by subject areas, such as biblical studies, music, medieval studies, renaissance studies, etc., these databases provide brief introductions to a given field, and are comprised of annotated peer-reviewed bibliographies of the best works in that particular field.

- *Oxford Dictionary of the Christian Church*. Because nobody can know everything about Christianity, Oxford invented the *Oxford Dictionary of the Christian Church*. The Antediluvian Librarians rarely go more than a day without consulting it.

- Religion and Philosophy Collection (also part of Academic Search Complete). Academic Search Complete is a broad-spectrum resource for articles on archaeology, history, psychology, and religion. The Religion and Philosophy Collection is a subset and is broader, but shallower, than ATLA Religion Database.

- *Westminster Dictionary of Theological Terms*. Another of the regular resources used by the Antediluvian Librarians, although your own pocket dictionary of theology will serve in most situations.

- WorldCat. WorldCat is a database consisting of catalogued items in libraries throughout North America and Western Europe. If you need to know if something exists, and who owns it, WorldCat will tell you. It will also generate bibliographic citations automatically in five scholarly styles, and it connects to Interlibrary Loan for ease of ordering.

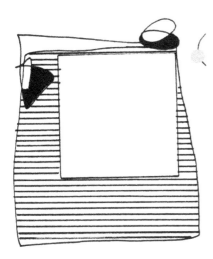

The Three Faces of Google

Google is like a powerful sorceress who gives you everything you ever ask for. But in doing that, is Google a good witch, a bad witch, or an indifferent witch? You have to judge for yourself.

Exercising good judgment when it comes to search engines, especially Google, is one of the keys to success in graduate school. Google is fast, easy, and (almost) intuitive. But are speed and volume a substitute for quality? In the early life of the Internet, faculty would answer that question with a resounding "No." These days, the answer is a bit more nuanced: "It depends" (often on advertising revenue rather than scholarly appropriateness). Therefore, it is up to you to perceive which results are appropriate for assignments and which are not. Google can be great, but it can also lead you astray. Most frequently its results fall somewhere in between and take you nowhere in particular.

You must ask yourself what is the most likely to make a professor wail and gnash her teeth or be dazzled by your perspicacity (look it up). And you must educate yourself, too. There are any number of excellent free web sites out there. Some of the Antediluvian Librarians' favorites include the Giza Archives Project from the Museum of Fine Arts in Boston, the American Methodism Digital Collection from the Duke Divinity Library and partner institutions, Bible Odyssey from the Society of Biblical Literature, and the Perseus Digital Library from Tufts University. In each of these cases you will notice that there is a respected institution standing behind, i.e. vouching for, the content they host. You can simply click on the "about" button to find out all about them.

In contrast, consider that Google can let you down badly with results that have no author's name or institutional affiliation. Who vouches for these sites? Why aren't they willing to stand behind the information they present? What is their agenda? Dodgy political opportunists, conspiracy theorists, and general cranks thrive in the netherworld of un-credited and un-affiliated web pages. Many groups with innocuous, even religious, sounding names can be wolves in sheep's clothing.

Another essential question to ask about results from Google is: *How dated is this information?* The question of age is particularly important when it comes to resources like Bible commentaries. For example, naïve students will sometimes use the commentaries of Matthew Henry that they find freely available online. These are fine for personal devotions, or even research papers on 17th and early 18th century theology, but not for basic exegesis. Why? Because Matthew Henry died in 1714. His commentaries are free online due to copyright law in the United States (https://copyright.cornell.edu/publicdomain). Consider the theological and biblical work that has been done in the 300 years since Henry's work came out. Do you want to base your exegetical essay on a source written before the development of universal human rights, individual liberty, germ theory, space travel, or the Beatles? Let alone the discovery of the Dead Sea Scrolls or the publication of critical editions of original language texts. Perhaps more current commentaries, like those your library provides in print and online, represent better choices, especially if you want to learn about and engage in current scholarly debates.

Therefore, use Google with discernment and learn to rely more heavily on the gold-standard resources that your institution purchases and maintains just for you. After all, you're worth it.

Primary, Secondary, and Tertiary Sources

What do professors mean when they talk about "primary" and "secondary" sources? It's as easy as one, two, three!

In theology, primary sources are the resources that come closest to an actual event, the first-hand or close-at-hand accounts of significant happenings or thoughts. It is information in its most unadulterated form, information that has not been interpreted, changed, or condensed from the time when it was recorded. For example, the Gospels are primary resources because they are as close as we can get to the actual words and actions of Jesus Christ. They were reported by eye-witnesses and handed down in the oral tradition until committed to paper (or papyrus). The works of Martin Luther represent another kind of primary source—the words of an actual religious leader, from his own sermons, lectures, and letters. The format in which the information appears does not matter. The writings and music of Hildegard of Bingen do not have to be in her own hand to count as a primary source; it can be her work in print, on a recording, and online. The critical aspect is that they are her own works.

Primary sources can also be accounts of historic events or people, or even objects and artifacts. Charles Wesley writing about John Wesley is a primary source for the life of John, because he was there. However, Charles Wesley writing about Jean Calvin would not be a primary source for the life of Jean Calvin, since they lived in different eras and different nations. Other types of primary resources include documentary film footage, voice recordings, and other types of electronic media from the past dozen decades. Newspapers, maps, original data sets like censuses or surveys, government documents, and even physical objects are primary sources. From the ancient world, we have coins, weapons, sculptures, painted pottery, and inscriptions in stone. From the middle ages, the Renaissance, and the early modern era, we have a wealth of material culture in museums, such as clothing, furniture, and portraiture. All of these can be primary sources because they capture something about a topic in the moment and communicate it directly to you without interference from any gatekeepers.

Secondary sources are the works that rest on the information provided by primary sources and try to make sense of it. They provide interpretation, analysis, and critical perspective, because they are created by leading scholars in a given field. For example, exegetical works are secondary sources, based on the primary information gleaned from the Bible, as well as many other sources. Similarly, biographies are secondary sources based on primary sources like memoirs, diaries, and letters.

Research articles, commentaries, and monographs (a book on a single topic) are all examples of secondary sources. They give us a comprehensive view of a topic, coming at it from many different perspectives, because secondary sources are not limited by space, time, or a single perspective. It is this aspect of secondary sources that make them useful for our own research; they help us make sense of a topic in ways that primary sources often cannot.

Tertiary sources organize and describe information from primary and secondary sources, and give quick, broad overviews of a topic. They rarely include original material. Examples of tertiary sources include subject-specific dictionaries and encyclopedias, like the *Oxford Dictionary of the Christian Church*, bibliographies, directories, and even some kinds of textbooks. Tertiary sources are exactly what you need when you are looking for quick useable information rather than nuanced interpretation. And as mentioned elsewhere, they are ideal for helping you to select a research topic efficiently.

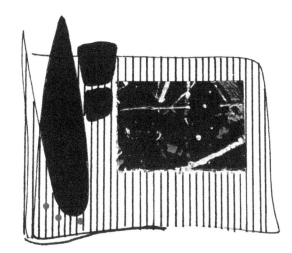

What Footnotes and Bibliographies Are Trying to Tell Us

Why is the formatting of footnotes and bibliographies so important, and what does it all mean?

Everyone struggles with formatting citations for footnotes and bibliographies, but there is a reason for standardizing styles. Your readers need to be able to tell what kind of source you are citing which, in turn, tells them where to look for it. Understanding the anatomy of citations allows you to distinguish one kind of resource from another—the formatting provides the clues. This is how a professor or a librarian can glance at a citation and tell you immediately where you will find it.

- Italics always indicate the title of the publication, whether it is a book or a journal.
- Quotation marks always denote an article in a journal or a chapter in a book.

Since the most commonly used scholarly style in seminary is Turabian (aka Chicago Humanities), we will describe the key elements for distinguishing one kind of citation from another for books and articles. For a more detailed discussion of what to look for, you can consult your style guide.

Books: You will see that the place of publication is included, as well as the name of the publisher. The only date present is the year. Book titles are always italicized.

> Taylor, Jeremy. *The Rule and Exercises of Holy Living: In Which Are Described the Means and Instruments of Obtaining Every Vertue, and the Remedies against Every Vice, and Considerations Serving to the Resisting All Temptations.* London: Printed by J.L. for T. Horne, J. Knapton, R. Knaplock, 1719.

Ebooks: The components are the same, with the addition of a URL. The URL can also indicate what platform hosts the resource.

> Taylor, Jeremy. *The Rule and Exercises of Holy Living.* Grand Rapids, MI: Christian Classics Ethereal Library, 1990. http://search.ebscohost.com/login.aspx?direct=true&scope=site&db=nlebk&db=nlabk&AN=2008330.

The titles of unpublished books (scholars sometimes share their manuscripts with colleagues prior to publishing them) appear in quotation marks, and "forthcoming" is used instead of a publication date.

The names of editors, translators, and compilers customarily follow the title, and are introduced with ed., trans., or comp. This is important to know since faculty have been known to refer to a famous work (such as Augustine's *City of God*) by the name of the person who translated their preferred edition.

Journal articles: You will see a title in quotation marks (article title) in addition to an italicized title (journal title). You will also see volume and issue numbers, page numbers, and dates that can include months or seasons. No publisher's name or place of publication is included. If the resource was published online, a URL will be present, and sometimes an access date, which is optional.

> Booty, John Everitt. "An Anglican Classic: Jeremy Taylor's Holy Living and Holy Dying." *Anglican Theological Review* 73, no. 2 (Spr 1991): 198–204.

Chapters within books: You will see a title in quotation marks (chapter title) in addition to an italicized title (book title). You will see the names of chapter author(s) and the book's editor(s). The place of publication is included, as well as the name of the publisher, the only date present is the year, and the book title is italicized. If the resource was published online, a URL will be present, and sometimes an access date, which is optional.

> Taylor, Jeremy. "The Rule and Exercises of Holy Living." In *Seventeenth-Century Verse and Prose*, edited by Helen Constance White, Ruth C. Wallerstein, and Ricardo Quintana, 167-95. New York: Macmillan, 1951.

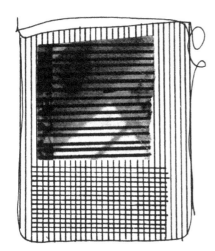

Wikipedia: Love It or Hate It, but Don't Cite It

Don't shortchange yourself with Wikipedia. Learn and embrace the standard reference works in theology to maximize the benefits of your education.

Ah, Wikipedia. Nothing raises hackles faster in academic circles than to speak its name. Yet Wikipedia is a tool, like any other. Just as you would not use a hammer to drill a hole or to trim a 2x4, you should only use Wikipedia appropriately. Sadly (for some), Wikipedia is highly inappropriate for use in academic work. The Antediluvian Librarians use the word "never" with reluctance, but our advice is to never, never, never cite Wikipedia in a scholarly research paper.

This statement bears repeating: ***never cite Wikipedia in a scholarly research paper.***

The principal objection to Wikipedia—and it's a strong one—is that the articles it presents are not attributed to an author. Nobody put their name on this work or stood up for the veracity of the information it presents. As far as anyone knows, the information could be false, or it could have been plagiarized from out-of-copyright sources (https://copyright.cornell.edu/publicdomain). Further, the articles have not undergone what is referred to as peer review. Peer review is exactly what the name says. When Professor E. X. Pert writes an encyclopedia article for Oxford University Press, the press sends it out to a few of his scholarly peers to assess it for its accuracy and value. These peers may suggest an insertion here or a rewrite there before the article is published. Or they may even reject it completely. By engaging in peer review, the author, the peers, and the press are all vouching that the end product is the very best and most accurate it can be.

Some students will argue that they find Wikipedia articles useful for their bibliographies. We applaud anyone delving deep enough into a topic to peruse bibliographies, but it must be done with a critical eye. Ask yourself whether the sources cited are up-to-date. Are any of them primary resources? Do they have the breadth and depth of serious research or do they mostly consist of other websites? Just for fun, run a few searches in Wikipedia. Now run those same searches in one, or more, of the resources offered by your institution, like the Oxford Handbooks or the *New Interpreter's Dictionary of the Bible*. Compare the results and decide for yourself which resource is richer.

The final, crucial, reason to avoid Wikipedia is this: if you rely on Wikipedia for your information needs in theology school, then you are not learning about, using, and relying upon the critical resources in your field. These resources include the databases, dictionaries, archives, and authors that you know to both trust and recommend to others. Since these are the very resources you will need for the remainder of your career, you are shortchanging yourself and cheapening your education. Heaven forbid that anyone asks you a penetrating question about a standard theological resource during a job interview.

For informal and non-academic research, Wikipedia is a wonderful thing. It can tell you quite a bit about the seasons and spinoffs of Project Runway, give a good account of how toothpaste becomes striped as its squeezed out of the tube, and provide decades' worth of baseball history and statistics for the majors, minors, semi-pros, college, youth, and little leagues. Wikipedia is extremely useful for casual conversations, trivia contests, and bar bets. However, you are safer going elsewhere for a discussion of John Wesley's understanding of grace, the Vatican's response to Liberation Theology, or the nuances of debate at the Ecumenical Councils.

Resources: Theological Research

Here are ten tips to keep in mind at the outset of a theological research project. With any luck, they will keep you sane, sensible, and successful.

Whenever possible try to select a topic or an area of research in which you are already interested, especially when working on a large project. It will hold your interest and take you further along the path toward where you want to be. The Antediluvian Librarians once heard a cynical dissertation advisor state that graduate students should choose topics with the same care that they would choose a spouse, because spouses come and go, but a thesis is forever.

Keyword searching in both the Library Catalog and subject databases is best for casting a broad net to catch any likely material suitable for your project. As you progress and gain a better feel for your subject, switch to more focused searches based on the names of authors, specific titles, or subject terms.

Students know what they call their topic, but that may not be what a Library Catalog or database is calling it. As you do your keyword searching, make note of the alternative terms and synonyms you see so that you can try for better results. Consulting various subject-specific dictionaries and encyclopedias will also yield good words and phrases for your research lexicon.

While we are discussing subject-specific dictionaries and encyclopedias . . . . Rather than checking out a stack of books on a subject you *might* want to research, search for your topic in the encyclopedias and dictionaries. These sources provide concise overviews of a topic along with reliable bibliographies for each article. They will help you to decide quickly and efficiently whether you like the topic. Then you can get the books.

Abbreviations in bibliographic citations are standard to each field and are customarily listed in the front matter of many reference works related to that field, especially those published by Oxford. (Knowing this fact alone will guarantee you genius status among your classmates and possibly even your TAs.)

There is no right way to keep your project organized—notecards, notebooks, word documents, bibliographic software—whatever system works for you is the one you should use. The important thing is to create and *maintain* the system where you store and access all the material you gather.

For large projects, create and maintain a checklist of tasks to help keep you focused. If it is a really large project, buy yourself a notebook or use a word document. Creating a timeline that includes both real and self-imposed deadlines can help keep you on track as well.

To save time and avoid accusations of plagiarism, when you take notes from sources always make note of the page number first. ***Always***. Next, and most importantly, is to always use quotation marks when pulling language verbatim from a source. "Teach this to your children, speaking about it when you sit at home, and when you walk along the road, when you lie down and when you get up. Write it on the doorposts or your houses and gates . . . ."

None of us knows when the resolution to a research problem will pop into our heads, so creating a way to capture these thoughts on the fly is essential. Smart phones, iPad apps, or plain old paper and pencil are equally good means of getting that idea down so you can retrieve it later. Do not kid yourself about remembering it; you won't.

While computer programs, databases, social media, and all sorts of other technologies deliver information with astounding rapidity, thought processes still take the same amount of time as they did in the days of Irenaeus of Lyons. Give yourself ample time to think about your project before you actually start writing; there are no short-cuts to this process.

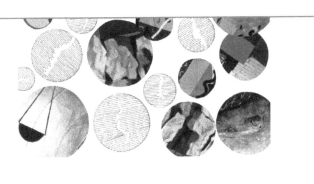

PART FIVE: WRITING – GETTING IT ON PAPER

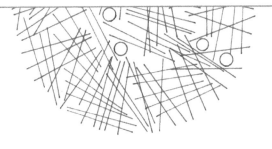

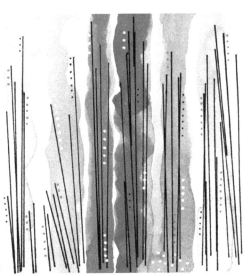

How Shall I Write Thee? Let Me Count the Ways

You will be expected to write in many different genres during your time in theology school. Understand the differences, be clear about what is expected, and seek help if you need it.

One aspect of seminary that hardly gets mentioned, or even considered, is the variety of genres, or styles, in which you are expected to write. If you had gone to law school or business school, you would write in the **single** style those disciplines expect of you. In Theology school, however, you are expected to communicate effectively in sermons, historical research papers (with footnotes), book reviews, exegetical papers (with footnotes), travel journals, spiritual formation journals, theological argument papers (with footnotes), reflection papers, and sometimes even hymns or poetry. It can be overwhelming as well as mystifying.

To avoid confusion about what kind of writing your professor expects, read the instructions for your assignment carefully. You might write the best reflection paper in the world, but if your assignment is for an exegesis paper, you will likely receive a poor grade. If instructions are not in the syllabus, a separate set of instructions should be forthcoming. If you are still confused, then ask your professors or TAs what kind of paper they expect. Remember, if you are baffled by something, chances are that your classmates are too. Seeking clarity on an assignment will also give you the opportunity to ask 1) whether the professors want to see reference notes and 2) if so, which scholarly citation style they prefer.

If you are feeling somewhat insecure about your ability to handle the writing demands of seminary, you have a number of resources at your disposal. Your librarians will be well-versed in the standard assignments and expectations at your institution. And now is a good time to investigate any writing support options that may be available. Both the library and the writing center may offer workshops aimed at helping you with your assignments. If all else fails, go online to see what kind of writing support is available from *reputable* institutions of higher learning, like other seminaries, theology schools, or universities.

You might also consider forming a writing accountability and support group from among your peers. The benefits will be working with people who have the same assignments and deadlines yet different strengths to bring to the table. Like study groups, this method can be effective as long as everyone is willing to commit to the discipline of the group.

Finally, several books exist to help with any writing perplexities. For example, Kate Turabian's *Manual for Writers of Research Papers, Theses, and Dissertations* covers more than just how to create a footnote. She touches on grammar, construction, punctuation, and spelling. Recent editions have been published online. Another option is to get yourself a copy of Strunk and White's *Elements of Style*. In 64 pages, the authors offer sage advice on writing with concision and clarity. This classic first appeared in the early 20th century and has not been out of print since. You can pick up a used copy for less than a medium-sized drink at Starbucks.

If all of these options seem time-consuming, they are. The key to success in writing is to be proactive. Many people argue that writing cannot be taught; you can only improve by doing it and getting feedback. Seminary provides the opportunity to do a lot of writing and get a lot of feedback. If you are feeling insecure about your writing, don't wait until the last minute to seek help. Find out about your options early, take advantage of them, and practice, practice, practice.

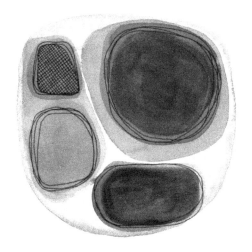

Selecting a Topic and Crafting a Thesis

Students can be daunted by the notion of having to come up with a topic and thesis for a research assignment, but the process is far less complicated than it seems. The trick is to give yourself time.

Don't kid yourself: finding a topic and crafting a thesis can be the toughest part of a writing project, regardless of the assignment. People seldom give themselves permission to take the time they need to be lost for a while. The Antediluvian Librarians urge you to be kind to yourself and think carefully about what subject area you'd like to work on—and do make sure it is something that interests you, because your life will be a misery if you have to work on something you hate.

Finding a topic and crafting a thesis begins with asking a good question. Where can you find a good question? You can start with your class notes and readings. Does anything stand out? Look for topics that speak to you in one way or another. In the course of the semester, what new bits of information have surprised you? Intrigued you? Irritated you? What do you wish the professor had explored further in the lectures? Is there an unresolved question from a classroom discussion that you'd like to pursue? Which readings engaged you? Which readings enraged you? Whose voices have been included and whose have been left out? These kinds of reflections will lead you to a thesis question.

Your thesis is your answer to the question you pose, that you will develop, explain, and defend in the body of your paper. Remember that a thesis represents the question that you hope to answer in the body of the paper. A scholarly paper is not a summary, it is an assertion (thesis) backed by evidence you find by doing research. To make an assertion is relatively simple. You take your question and restate it as a sentence. You will eventually prove or disprove your thesis statement using the evidence you gather in your research. Therefore, looking for questions is crucial. Your analysis of the information you collect in your research will provide the answer to your question, i.e. your thesis. A good thesis will invite more questions, like why or how. You can begin your research by looking for the answers to those questions, and use these subsidiary questions to structure your paper.

When trying to craft a thesis, it often helps to talk out an idea with a receptive listener, or to diagram your ideas on paper using bullet points, pictures, mind maps, multi-colored markers, or anything else that unlocks your thought processes. Once you have your question—try to recast the question as a statement. Your thoughts may be rough or ridiculous at first, but if you keep at it, you can refine your ideas until you have something to work with. For example, the process might look like this:

Initial Questions: Is it even worth slogging through boring old hierarchical Aquinas? The dude's been dead for centuries. Don't newer theologians make better sense for people today?

Refined question: Does Aquinas have anything significant to say to modern readers about the existence and revelation of God to humanity, and how does his work compare with more recent theologians?

Question rephrased as a thesis statement: Aquinas provides insights into the existence and revelation of God to humanity that may or may not compare favorably with more recent theologians, but still offer significant insights for today's readers.

Finally, once you have a thesis with which to work, try not to force your evidence to fit into its mold. Instead, listen to what the evidence tells you and allow your thesis to evolve. This evolution is called a research cycle. You begin with a question, formulate the thesis, do some research and reflecting, then refine your question/thesis. Going through the research cycle again and again moves you from the beginning of a project through to completion. Keep track of the evolution of your thesis, because it can provide a nice introduction to your work. For example, you could say that based on what you knew previously, the situation appeared to be one thing, whereas in light of the evidence, it is actually something different. Then introduce your revised thesis statement. Effective engagement with the research process will lead you to new insights and knowledge; it could even lead to you to regard Aquinas with new respect.

Introducing Structure

Create an outline for each of your papers and use it like a roadmap: to remember the right direction, to stick to the topic under discussion, and to arrive safely at your destination.

Unless you are writing a journal, most of the writing you will be required to do in theology school will require a beginning, a middle, and an end, i.e. an introduction, a body, and a conclusion. Arranging your words in a logical progression at the paragraph level, at the essay level, and at the thesis level allows you to keep your arguments and evidence in order and also helps your reader to follow what you are trying to convey. Unlike everyday conversation, where we skitter haphazardly from one topic to the next, effective formal writing needs structure.

The best way to introduce structure into our writing is to plan ahead by creating an outline, or a mind map, or a checklist of topics we want to cover in order to support our thesis. The thesis lets the reader know where this writing is going to go, like using a roadmap to drive to Cleveland. With the map a driver might actually get to Cleveland. Without directions, she might forget a critical turn and wind up in Pittsburgh; without an outline, you might forget a critical point and wind up with a flawed argument. For example, if you were writing a short essay on John Wesley, you might create an outline like this:

> *Thesis:* John Wesley was concerned for the poor and prisoners from the earliest days of his ministry
> *Introduction:* Set the stage for Wesley and lay out thesis
> *Body paragraph #1:* Formation of the Holy Club at Oxford and their activities
> *Body paragraph #2:* Impact of poverty and debtors' prisons in Wesley's life as well as in 18th century British society
> *Body paragraph #3:* Ongoing activities in support of the destitute and imprisoned
> *Conclusion:* Restate thesis and reiterate why the three pieces of evidence discussed support it

The topic sentence of each paragraph is like a mini thesis. It should introduce the idea of each paragraph. The body of the paragraph provides supporting details (like evidence and analysis of the evidence) and links the paragraph back to the paper's overall thesis. This helps to keep the overall project on track and prevents you from introducing unrelated material in that section. All reasons, explanations, and details related to the topic sentence of a particular paragraph should go in that paragraph. If they are not relevant to that paragraph's main point, then they need to go in a different paragraph.

Finally, there is the issue of knitting all the parts together to form a seamless whole. Transitioning neatly from one paragraph to the next does not need to be a labored process. Transitions move the reader forward along the path of your argument easily with no bumps or potholes. You will see from your assigned reading that there are any number of short transition words and phrases to help you do this. Here are some examples:

Similarly
In contrast
Like the above
In addition
In conclusion
Related to this idea
Moreover
Alternatively
Unlike
Rather than
Nevertheless
Consequently

The Critical Importance of Lousy First Drafts

Don't let your first draft be your final draft!

Would you serve rare turkey at Thanksgiving? Would you publicly perform a Christmas carol you had practiced only once? Would you walk down the aisle in a wedding dress held together with pins? Of course not. Then why would you turn in a first draft of a paper?

First drafts are an essential part of the process of writing, and they are universally awful. A first draft allows you to get something on paper to work with. It's the unrefined ore of the gold mine in your brain. You dig out the material, select the most promising bits, heat them or subject them to various chemical processes, and at the end, you will have gotten to the pure substance that you (and your professor) seek. First drafts, by definition, are disorganized, illogical, and filled with false starts and errors. They take unexpected detours away from the thesis statement, get stuck on tangents, and lose steam long before arriving at a conclusion.

The good news is that first drafts are only first drafts. You can always go back and improve them, *cough* if you leave yourself enough time *cough*. In fact, writing experts suggest that it is better to write your first draft straight through, without stopping to fix anything, rather than starting again and again, or getting stuck picking apart one poor sentence. They make this suggestion for two reasons: first, you get a whole draft completed and, second, you often won't have a clear idea of your conclusion until you actually get there. Boldly write your first draft from start to finish, then see where you are at the end. That way you'll have the elation that comes from actually having written it to carry you through the process of revising it.

Once you have your first draft in front of you, **do not turn it in**. Instead, let it sit for a day and go back to it with fresh eyes. You will then see it as a whole and make better decisions about how to improve it. Our essay on "Finishing Touches" delves into this process, and introduces the idea that you should invest at least 25% of the time you budget for writing in **re-**writing. This time allows you to grapple with the nuances that complex topics require. You can fill in the blank spots, expand ideas, clarify examples, and doctor your transitions. Drafting gives you innumerable opportunities to improve your organization and word choices, while tending to your paper's faulty mechanics. Ideas and errors alike will leap out and demand your attention. The more time you let a paper rest between drafts, the more this will happen, and the happier you will be with the final product.

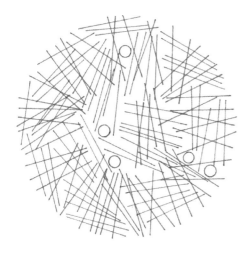

An Ode to Strunk & White

To demonstrate just how antediluvian the Antediluvian Librarians are, here is our paean to a literary gem first published over one hundred years ago. Nevertheless, it remains amazingly useful today (The Elements of Style, *not the doggerel below*).

Every field, discipline, and genre has its classics: chocolate chip cookies, the Ford Mustang, Ella Fitzgerald, and the 1927 Yankees. For beginning, intermediate, and advanced writers, the pinnacle of good advice is *The Elements of Style* by William Strunk, Jr. and E. B. White. It is 105 pages of sensible, easy-to-follow guidance on making your writing crisp, clear, and correct. Better still, the current retail price on Amazon is a whopping $6, and it's probably much less at your area's used book store. We promise that you'll get better value out of it than a similarly priced caramel macchiato (and it won't go straight to your hips).

This gem first appeared in 1918 and has remained in print ever since. It covers most of the issues that vex us: grammar, usage, spelling, and principles of good composition. It identifies commonly misused expressions and offers a glossary for anyone who is baffled by terms such as "participle" or "predicate," which makes it doubly useful for students of foreign languages. It can be read straight through or dipped into for reference. Everyone can benefit from this book—take it from those of us who also staff a Theological Writing Center.

The title of this column promises an ode, so here goes:

"Omit needless words," say Strunk and White.
"Use active voice; keep sentences tight."
Rare advice in these days of Facebook and text,
When grammarians weep, and professors are vexed.

This one little book stands for order and meaning.
Buy it at once and then begin gleaning
Its nuggets of Truth, examples of Clarity,
Then write better papers from love and from charity.

For T.A.s will bless you, and faculty cheer
All those crisp concise sentences and essays so clear.

Resources: Our Favorite Books on Writing

Casagrande, June. *Grammar Snobs Are Great Big Meanies: A Guide to Language for Fun and Spite.* New York: Penguin Books, 2006.

Core, Deborah. *The Seminary Student Writes.* St. Louis, MO: Chalice Press, 2000.

Gordon, Karen Elizabeth. *The Deluxe Transitive Vampire: The Ultimate Handbook of Grammar for the Innocent, the Eager, and the Doomed.* New York: Pantheon Books, 1993.

Griffin, Simon. *F___ing Apostrophes: A Guide to Show You Where You Can Stick Them.* London: Icon Books, 2016.

Lamott, Anne. *Bird by Bird: Some Instructions on Writing and Life.* New York: Anchor Books, 1995.

Silvia, Paul J. *How to Write a Lot: A Practical Guide to Productive Academic Writing.* Washington, DC: American Psychological Association, 2007.

Strunk, William, and E. B. White. *The Elements of Style.*

Truss, Lynne. *Eats, Shoots & Leaves: The Zero Tolerance Approach to Punctuation.* New York: Gotham Books, 2004.

Turabian, Kate L. *A Manual for Writers of Research Papers, Theses, and Dissertations: Chicago Style for Students and Researchers.* Chicago: University of Chicago Press, 2007.

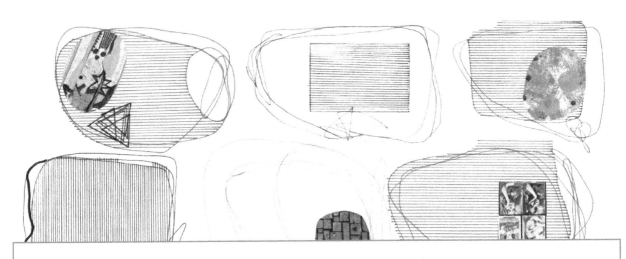

PART SIX: WRITING MECHANICS — MAKING IT PRETTY AND CORRECT

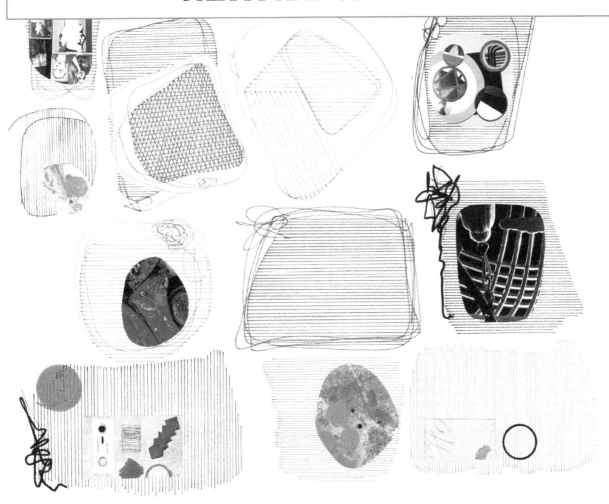

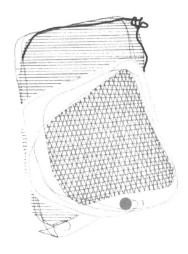

Grammar, Spelling, and Punctuation

Accuracy is a worthy goal for any writer. Take the time and care necessary to make your work as error free as possible.

The time has come to raise the issue of accuracy in spelling, grammar, and punctuation. The Antediluvian Librarians understand your feelings: proper mechanics are a pain. Nobody communicating on social media these days bothers about it, so why is it important? We are so glad you asked. First and foremost, isn't it worth taking extra care when you are representing and communicating the word of God? Shouldn't you strive for precision in matters of faith? After all, your congregation and your readers are relying on you.

When your readers notice that you are not exercising care with the details of your writing—that you didn't bother to proofread your work before putting it out there, or that spell check let a few homophones slip through—they might start to wonder about larger issues. In other words, they might come to believe that mistakes with your commas, quotation marks, modifiers, and tenses translate into mistakes with your theology. They also might wonder why they are taking the time to read something that you didn't take the time to correct. It's a question of trust. Lose your reader's trust and you will have a very hard time getting it back.

If you are feeling especially shaky about your grasp of writing mechanics, you will want to consult a more comprehensive resource than what we offer here. In the meantime, we present a list of some of the most common problems that crop up in student papers:

- In formal writing, especially theology where accuracy is paramount to conveying meaning, contractions (don't, can't, shouldn't) and abbreviations should be avoided. The only exceptions are for abbreviating versions of the Bible (e.g., NRSV, NKJ) and journal titles if you use SBL style.

- Verbs should correctly reflect the number of subjects, and their tenses should be consistent.

- Know the difference between such common homophones as

  o To, two, and too

  o There, their, and they're

○ Its and it's—see upcoming section on apostrophes

- Keep a dictionary at hand and form the habit of using it in conjunction with spell check. Don't rely solely on spell check.

- Create a habit of using good grammar and correct spelling in all your communications—even Twitter.

- In the United States, punctuation goes inside the quotation mark at the end of a sentence. Example: ". . . and the angels waited on him."

- Reference notes follow all other punctuation at the end of sentences. While it is technically permissible to place them in the middle of a sentence, it is better for the flow of your prose if you don't. Example: ". . . and the angels waited on him."[1]

- Semicolons and commas perform two distinct jobs and should not be used interchangeably. The Antediluvian Librarians argue that one is either born knowing how to use a semicolon or one is not; there is no middle ground. If semicolons confuse you, simply avoid them. Many successful people have lived happy, useful lives without ever bothering with semicolons.

- Colons are used before a list, between chapter and verse in Bible references, and in any situation where the word "namely" might be used. If it makes sense to use "namely," or "specifically," or "especially," etc., then it is acceptable to use a colon.

- Quotations within quotations (nested quotes) are denoted with a single quotation mark. Example: Prof. Jones said, "Pay particular attention to the section where John Paul II says, 'The future starts today, not tomorrow.'"

- Do not begin a sentence with a numeral. Either spell the number out, or precede it with a modifier. Example: "First Corinthians, chapter 2: 5, states . . ." or "The verse in the second chapter of I Corinthians states. . ." never "1 Corinthians states . . ."

- Exclamation points do not enhance scholarly essays. Hold them in reserve for social media posts, congratulatory segments of church newsletters, and baby announcements.

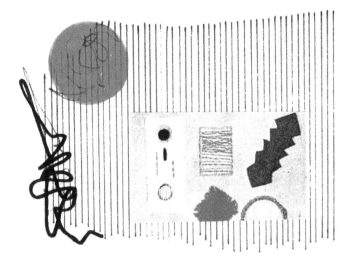

A Special Note on Apostrophes

Apostrophes—the struggle is real.

Apostrophes get their own discussion because they confuse everyone, as public signage throughout the English-speaking world demonstrates. Google *apostrophe mistakes* if you don't believe us. In the spirit of clarity, therefore, we are offering a few tips on how to manage this especially vexing piece of punctuation:

First, apostrophes **never** denote the plural of a noun. You can safely disregard all signs proclaiming the presence of "donut's," "dvd's," or "tire's." Next, the original purpose of an apostrophe was to indicate the absence of a letter. This is why you write "don't" for "do not," "it's" for "it is," and "couldn't" for "could not." Except that one should never use contractions like these in scholarly papers.

> Apostles = more than one apostle
> Jesus said the apostles shouldn't linger in an unwelcoming village.

If that were all there was to it, most of us would be fine. Sadly, the poor overworked apostrophe is burdened with the additional task of denoting possessives, and here is where the English language descends into anarchy. It's scary, but please read on . . . .

In the case of a simple possessive, the apostrophe marks the possessive of a singular noun, such as "the dog's food." It also marks the possessive of a plural noun not ending in "s," such as "the women's bathroom," or "the children's playground."

> Apostle's = belonging to an apostle
> The apostle's robe should be warm enough.

But wait, there's more . . . An apostrophe can mark the possessive of a plural noun that does end in "s." But here you put the apostrophe after the "s" not before. So, if you ran an overcrowded shelter for Siberian Eelhounds, you would refer to "the dogs' food," and "the cages' floors." Then there are the singular nouns that end in "s," which can go either way, depending on your personal preference: "the hem of Jesus's robe" or "the hem of Jesus' robe."

> The apostles' fear of reprisals drove them to the upper room.
> Jesus' tomb was empty when the apostles went to check on it.

The last straw in this incredible scenario is "its." Because "its" is the only instance in which you do not use an apostrophe to denote the possessive. It's completely confusing and the only thing to do is memorize the rule.

It's hard to believe that Jerusalem and all its inhabitants demanded Jesus' crucifixion.

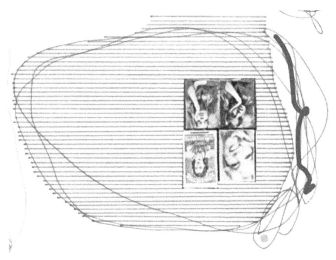

Active vs. Passive Voice Verbs

The real power in writing rests not in adjectives as some students suppose, but in the verbs. Cultivate active and lively verbs to lend your writing a punch and hold passive voice constructions in reserve for your parish council minutes.

Faculty often urge students to avoid the passive voice in their writing, but sometimes what this means confuses us. Passive voice is not the same thing as past tense, which we use to describe something that has already happened. Passive voice, on the other hand, means constructing the sentence in such a way that the subject is acted upon by the object. If the subject of your sentence is a cat, and the object is a mouse, then here is an example:

> *Past tense*: The cat ate the mouse.
> *Passive voice*: The mouse was eaten by the cat.

Another way of describing it is a sentence that depends on the verb "to be." By using a construction involving is, was, were, etc., you dilute the impact of your main descriptive verb and make your sentence wordier. This is a pretty unsatisfactory explanation, so here is an example to illustrate the problem:

> *Passive:* Sisera <u>was</u> killed instantly when a tent peg that <u>was</u> seized by Jael <u>was</u> driven into his skull.
> *Active:* Seizing the tent peg, Jael drove it through Sisera's skull, killing him instantly.

If you think the second sentence sounds more action-packed than the first, you've got the idea. Active voice is for speakers and novelists; passive voice is for bureaucrats. Action verbs enliven your writing and keep people engaged; passive voice constructions are the rhetorical equivalent of C-SPAN. If you remain confused, there is always another alternative. Try adding the words "by zombies" to the end of your sentence. If the sentence still reads correctly then you've used passive voice: the mice were eaten by zombie cats.

Don't get us wrong, there is a time and place for using passive voice—usually where you are trying to convey that something major happened yet not name names. Consider your church's annual report to the bishop. Which of these two options is more merciful?

Active: Mr. I. M. Feckless destroyed the parish hall kitchen when he accidentally drove his Buick through the wall. We rebuilt it once his insurance company paid.

Passive: The parish hall kitchen was destroyed when a Buick was accidentally driven through the wall. It was rebuilt after the insurance settlement was paid.

Remember to use passive voice if you don't want Mr. Feckless to take the blame for a kitchen remodel that the whole parish wanted anyway. After all, his insurance paid for the work.

But let's get back to active verbs. Active verbs grab a reader's attention. They give your work clarity, concision, and they don't pussyfoot around. Plus, they make professors happy. For example, look at the possible substitutions for this sentence: "Many of the Romans were persuaded by Paul's soteriological promise."

- Paul's soteriological promise convinced them.

- Paul's soteriological promise enchanted them.

- Paul's soteriological promise swayed them.

If your writing lacks verve, embrace active verbs. Cultivate them, collect them, and use them; there are lots to go around.

The active verbs contributing to this essay include:

Confuse	Enchant	Kill	Rest
Convince	Engage	Lend	Seize
Cultivate	Enliven	Pay	Sound
Destroy	Give	Pussyfoot	Sway
Dilute	Grab	Read	Try
Drive	Hold	Rebuild	Urge

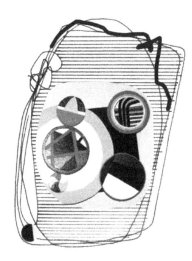

My What Is Dangling?

"One morning I shot an elephant in my pajamas. How he got into my pajamas, I'll never know."
Groucho Marx, *Animal Crackers* (1930)

Dangling modifiers happen when a writer inadvertently disconnects a phrase or clause from the word they intended it to modify, often with humorous results. Logic suggests that Groucho was in his pajamas when he shot the elephant, yet the actual word order reads otherwise—hence the joke. Rarely does a student paper cross the desks of the Antediluvian Librarians that does not contain one or more examples of a dangling modifier. However, rather than going into the nitty gritty of grammatical rules and terminology (both complicated and unhelpful) we offer the following examples of dangling modifiers with suggestions on how to correct them. By raising your awareness that these things lurk in the dark corners of first drafts, perhaps you can begin recognizing and fixing the problem before it shows up in a sermon, church newsletter, or other public forum.

- Pharaoh's daughter discovered baby Moses bathing in the river. => Pharaoh's daughter discovered baby Moses as she bathed in the river.

- Removing his shoes, the burning bush spoke to Moses. => Moses removed his shoes, and the burning bush spoke to him.

- Pharaoh's men chased the Israelites driving chariots. => Driving chariots, Pharaoh's men chased the Israelites.

- Stretching out his hand, the Red Sea parted for Moses. => Moses stretched out his hand, and the Red Sea parted.

- Sacrificing to the golden calf, Moses came down from the mountain. => Moses came down from the mountain to find the Israelites sacrificing to the golden calf.

- Dying before reaching the Promised Land, Joshua led the people into Canaan. => Moses died before reaching the Promised Land, leaving Joshua to lead the people into Canaan.

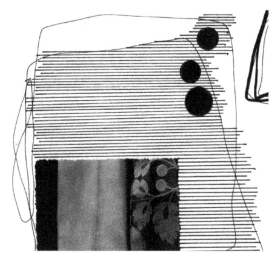

Finishing Touches

*Many of us mistakenly assume that our papers are complete once we have finished putting words on paper. On the contrary, **at least 25% of the time** we budget for a writing assignment should involve re-writing, editing, proofreading, etc.*

If St. Peter required a written essay before he'd open the pearly gates and let us into Heaven, you can bet that we would all sweat every last detail and make that essay as perfect as we possibly could. Yet when it comes to class assignments, many of us are satisfied with dashing something off without another thought and then moving on to the next thing. Our grades reflect this, because the one thing that Prof. Long-in-the-Tooth can recognize after decades in the classroom is a sloppy first draft.

The time and attention students expend on their written assignments are inevitably reflected in their grades. If you want a good grade, then you have to invest in the post-writing process: go over your writing carefully, tweak it here and there, gasp in horror, and then correct that egregious error you accidentally incorporated. Polish your prose like the shoes of a Marine Colonel about to go on dress parade. This is what real writers do, and it's the care they lavish on their words after they are put on the page that separates the Hemingways from the amateurs. It takes time and practice, and you don't want to go to the other extreme of fixating on one small bit of your writing to the detriment of the whole. If you want to be a good writer, however, attention to detail is key to the process. There are no shortcuts.

When time is short, at least leave enough wiggle room to go back over your work and fix the mechanical issues, such as subject-verb agreement, consistent verb tenses, spelling errors, etc. Read it aloud to yourself or, since people often have trouble spotting the errors in their own work, ask a friend or family member to read and correct your papers for you. Remember to reward them for doing it. It's amazing how much help you can get for the price of a Starbucks gift card or a pizza. If you plan to do the polishing yourself, then here are the things to bear in mind beyond simple mechanics. This list could go on and on, but we will leave it at our top ten:

1. Do you have a clear thesis statement and does your evidence support it?

2. Does each paragraph have a topic sentence, and does it relate to the rest of the paragraph?

3. Does your argument flow in a logical order?

4. Do you have an introduction and a conclusion and do they agree with one another?

5. Are you happy with your word choices? Have you used the same term(s) repeatedly?

6. Have you included footnotes for all your quotations? And have you footnoted key concepts that came from somebody other than yourself?

7. Is there repetition that you can eliminate to make your work tighter and more direct?

8. Are there wiggle words and meaningless phrases that are acting as filler?

9. Are you relying on several Big Block Quotations strung together with very few of your own sentences?

10. Are you using passive voice constructions rather than active verbs?

Favorite Resources for Writing

An unabridged dictionary—for obscure and not-commonly-used words

Casagrande, June. *Grammar Snobs Are Great Big Meanies: A Guide to Language for Fun and Spite*. New York: Penguin Books, 2006.

The Chicago Manual of Style, 17th Edition. University of Chicago Press, 2017.

Collins, Billie Jean. *The SBL Handbook of Style*. Atlanta, GA: SBL Press, 2014.

Gordon, Karen Elizabeth. *The Deluxe Transitive Vampire: The Ultimate Handbook of Grammar for the Innocent, the Eager, and the Doomed*. New York: Pantheon Books, 1993.

Gorman, Michael J. *Elements of Biblical Exegesis: A Basic Guide for Students and Ministers*. Peabody, MA: Hendrickson Publishers, 2009.

Griffin, Simon. *F——ing Apostrophes: A Guide to Show You Where You Can Stick Them*. London: Icon Books, 2016.

Lamott, Anne. *Bird by Bird: Some Instructions on Writing and Life*. New York: Anchor Books, 1995.

OED—The Oxford English Dictionary, for the meaning and history of words, past and present. Most institutions will have access to this resource online.

Silvia, Paul J. *How to Write a Lot: A Practical Guide to Productive Academic Writing*. Washington, DC: American Psychological Association, 2007.

Strunk, William, and E. B. White. *The Elements of Style*. Boston: Allyn and Bacon, 2000.

Thesaurus.com. Some folks will argue in favor of Dictionary.com as well, but we prefer **unabridged** dictionaries.

Truss, Lynne. *Eats, Shoots & Leaves: The Zero Tolerance Approach to Punctuation*. London: Profile Books, 2003.

Our Favorite Real-Life Spell Czech Misses

You can see a lot of comical errors when you offer writing support to a theology school over many years. Here we have listed some of our favorites, collected from 2013 to 2019. We offer them as an illustration of why you cannot rely solely on spell check. On the left is what our writers meant to say. On the right you will see how spell check allowed it to appear on the page.

brother	brothel
canon	cannon
denomination	demonization
eschatological	scatological
euthanasia	youth in Asia
faith and reason	faith and treason
hierarchy	hire Archie
hypothesis	hypostasis
liberation	liberalization
pericope	periscope
pneuma	pneumonia
revelation	revolution
St. Augustine of Hippo	St. Augustine of Hip Hop
systematic theology	systemic theology

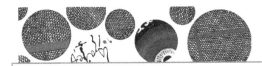

PART SEVEN: THE HARD STUFF

Pacing Yourself for Larger Papers

Trying to dash a large paper off at the last minute will do neither your grades nor your health any good. Organization, determination, and dedication are required for conquering a lengthy project.

In case it has not yet become apparent, the idea of theological writing as a leisurely and meditative activity is something of a myth in seminary. Large spaces of time in which to ponder life, the universe, and everything rarely fall into our laps. If they do, they are likely to be accompanied by dental emergencies, car trouble, or a backed-up sewer line in the parish hall the day before Easter. Is it any wonder that St. Jerome found a nice quiet cave in which to translate the Vulgate?

With all the intrusions of everyday life, how can we manage a large research paper, or even a thesis? Here are some ideas we hope you find useful:

- You have to fight for time to write. Nobody will give it to you and very few people will make it easy to hang onto. This is battle, folks. You want it? Come and take it.

- Start early. Get organized as soon as you can, and then work to stay organized. Create an outline for the paper and a timeline for your writing. Whatever it takes and however you want to do it. Just do it.

- Do a little bit of work each week. You'll be amazed at how quickly the body of your work builds up into something significant.

- In the same vein, try to do whatever you can in the little snippets of time you get: in your child's carpool line, waiting at the pharmacy, or during the pre-game show at sporting events. You will be amazed at how many sentences you can knock out in the time it takes to check Facebook.

- Keep a method of recording your thoughts with you at all times so you don't lose that brilliant insight.

- Plan what you want to say before you sit down at the computer. You can do this while exercising, showering, whatever. Think through enough of your project to have an inkling of where it's going to take you.

- Structure is essential. If you don't have one assigned, then create one. And don't underestimate the time it takes to do that.

- Sync your assignments. As much as possible, try to relate your research assignments so that you can borrow research done in one for another. Example: the exegetical paper you're doing on the letters of Paul might have bearing on some aspect of your systematic theology paper. This does **not** mean, however, that one paper can or should be submitted for different classes.

- Schedule time for serious re-writing and editing. A first draft is only a first draft. Create a second draft and then schedule a time to ask somebody to review your work.

- The person you ask to review your work should have solid writing skills. And you must always reward them: fancy coffee, a pizza, help with moving, or baby- and pet-sitting are some examples of suitable compensation.

Scholarly Citations and Plagiarism

A great deal of confusion exists about scholarly citations and plagiarism, but it is essential for students to familiarize themselves with the intricacies of these so they don't fall into inadvertent error. Your institution's librarians or writing center are resources you can always consult when in doubt.

Contrary to popular belief, professors do not insist on correct scholarly citations simply to torture poor overworked seminarians. Citations actually serve two important functions. First, they allow readers to see where specific information came from (and if you are revisiting some of your earlier work, that reader could be you). Next, they give credit where credit is due to the scholars on whose shoulders you are standing—both for direct quotations and for ideas, theories, or concepts that did not originate with you, thereby avoiding plagiarism. Correct citations are the hallmark of the ethical, the courteous, and the responsible—all desirable characteristics in ministry.

Because the notion of what constitutes plagiarism varies across different cultures, the Antediluvian Librarians frequently meet with student confusion about when and why to cite something. Generally speaking,

- You **do not** need to create a footnote for information that is common knowledge among your intended audience of readers.

- You **do** need to create a footnote when your paper includes a direct quotation from another source.

- You **do** need to create a footnote when your paper includes an idea, theory, or concept that another person came up with—even if that idea or concept is not presented as a quotation. In other words, if you are summarizing someone else's contribution to a theological debate, you still need to cite the source.

While there are hundreds, if not thousands, of different styles for handling the formatting of notes and bibliographies, the best way of dealing with citation styles is to select the style that works for you and is the standard in your discipline or institution. Memorize three or four of the most common types of formatting in that style, and keep its style manual close at hand for ready reference—we keep ours adjacent to our study Bible, our dictionary of theological terms, and our *Oxford Dictionary of the Christian Church*. Alternatively, you can use an automatic citation generator, but ***you still need to know*** *the most common formats in your style of choice so that you can proofread your citations* to confirm that they are correct. Many databases now offer the option of creating a citation for you, or you might decide to investigate bibliographic software products, which is a particularly good idea if you plan on an academic career. Popular options include Zotero, RefWorks, or EndNote. Regardless of how they are generated, always remember to check your citations for accuracy.

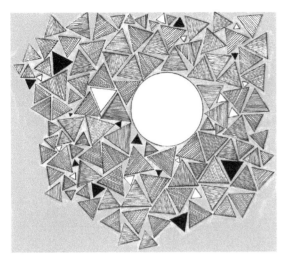

Preparing for Exams

When it comes to exams, cramming is never a good strategy.

All-nighters, excessive caffeine, cramming . . . research indicates most of what we learn through these methods is soon forgotten. The anxiety and loss of sleep associated with cramming can actually lead to poorer exam performance. So what should we do?

- Relax and breathe. Anxiety is a hindrance. Try to gain perspective and practice stress management. If you're starting to clench, take a walk around the building to get your blood circulating.

- Nothing beats regular study, but if you haven't been keeping up with your coursework, don't give up or panic; make a plan now. Set aside time to study and devise a strategy to review the material that the exam will cover.

- Listen to your instructor. He or she will almost certainly tell you which material the exam will include and what kind of analysis is expected. The course syllabus is also a reliable roadmap. Use it to help you plan your study.

- Create outlines, diagrams, lists of key concepts, and concept maps as part of your review process. They will help you organize your thinking as well as remember content.

- While no one can learn it for you, you may find it helpful to work with a study partner or group. Unless you are an introvert, in which case do your own thing.

- Use flashcards, practice exams, or create your own top-ten lists of things to know as alternative methods for processing and retaining information.

- Practice good self-care. Eat a healthy diet. Get regular exercise. Take it easy with the caffeine and get a good night's sleep before the exam. Research indicates that overall good health and being alert and clearheaded produces better exam performance than all-nighters and artificial stimulants.

Writer's Block

*Don't let writer's block stand in the way of getting your work done. Remember that 90% of writing is **re-writing**, so do what you can to get something, anything down on paper.*

You need to write an essay. You have blocked out time to get started. You have turned your back on the blue skies and delicious breezes outside. You have resolved your current domestic dilemmas and the household is at peace. You turn to your computer screen with the best intentions in the world, open a blank document, rest your fingers on the keyboard, and . . . . Nothing. Comes. Out.

Writer's block has nothing to do with one's experience or abilities; it comes to everyone, like the common cold. Feeling stressed is one cause. Others include thinking about too many things at once, inability to focus, or insufficient research. Rather than examining the causes of the problem, though, let's look at some solutions.

Everyone knows the common cures such as talking it through, taking a walk, or engaging in some other distracting activity for a short time. Here are some not-so-common ideas that may help:

- Rant. If you are feeling the pressure, sit down and type a rant. Include all the things that are bugging you. Use bad language. This technique not only removes all the clutter from your brain, it allows you to view it in black and white thereby diminishing its hold over you.

- Zone out. Take five minutes to sit perfectly still. Close your eyes and focus on your breathing. Do nothing else. Five minutes is actually a lot longer than you think, and it can help stop Brain Frenzy in its tracks.

- Get messy. Just start writing anything at all that comes to you—the nonsense, the drivel, whatever. You should even—it pains us to say—forget about spelling, grammar, organizational structure, or staying inside the lines. Let yourself go. Once you get something down on paper you can go back and fix it.

- Switch implements. Write with a tool different from what you usually use. Use a pen and paper if you normally use a computer. Text yourself bits and pieces that you can pull together later. Find an empty classroom and use the white board. Shifting your physical routine will throw you off balance just enough to get your brainwaves flowing.

- Switch writing venues. Find an environment that is the opposite of where you normally work.

- Write about your writer's block. You can even make it a letter to your professor in which you list all the things you would have said if writer's block had not prevented you.

- Use images to get started. Grab a theological art book, access your institution's art databases, or grab your phone to look on Pinterest. Pictures that relate to your topic can elicit emotional and creative responses that can unlock your thoughts.

- Try starting your paper in the middle or the second point. Introductions and conclusion are the last things to write anyway, so ignore them and feel free to begin anywhere.

- Copy and paste or type out potentially relevant quotations to get over the hump of a blank page.

- Review your notes and readings from class. It may be that you don't yet have a clear understanding of the topic and your confusion is bogging you down.

Don't let writer's block get the better of you. Find ways to tame it that work for you, so that you don't have to worry about it anymore. Just knowing you have techniques in your arsenal can help.

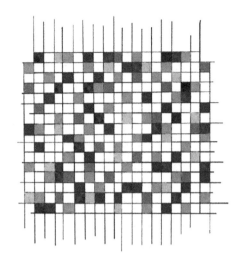

Creating an Organizational System for Life

Finding a solid organizational system that works well for you is totally worth the investment of time. Look for one that is simple, flexible, and can last throughout your career.

What topic could be closer to the hearts of the Antediluvian Librarians than that of systems for storing and retrieving information? Ah, bliss! However, this is not just an important topic for professional organizers; it applies to anyone undertaking graduate education.

If you have not considered this topic before, then now is the time. Why? Because theology school is the place where tons of information is coming at you, fast and furious: class notes, required reading, suggested reading, research projects, sermons, church newsletters, emails, texts, social media posts, etc. To conjure a metaphor from our beloved New Orleans, it's as if the Celestial Corps of Engineers allowed a breach in the Industrial Canal of Theology, causing the 9th Ward of our brains and offices to overflow with a toxic soup of TMTI—Too Much Theological Information. "But," you are correct in asserting, "it's good stuff. I will probably want to refer to later in my career. I just need to get it under control." We agree, so here are some preliminary ideas for how you can do just that.

First, take a little time now to review what systems are available. These days there is a system or program to fit just about every need, some of them free, some of them quite expensive. Some of them are easy to use, others have a steep learning curve. If you Google "systems for organizing notes," you will get everything from hacks for keeping notes on paper, to using the Cornell System, all the way through digital systems like Evernote. The same holds for bibliographic management systems, which range from index cards, to Zotero (free), to ProCite (expensive). There is truly a system out there for everyone. Or maybe six. Or sixty.

To approach this subject without losing your mind at the breadth of choices, create a list of features you believe will be important to you. Be realistic. Very few of us need a system so powerful that it can launch rockets. Ask around. Your professors and friends will usually have recommendations. No system is perfect, but you want to choose something with reasonable flexibility and longevity. Determining your own list of essential features will help you wade through the jungle of options. Things to ask yourself might include:

- Am I comfortable using this system?

- Will I use this system consistently?

- Will it accommodate my changing needs over the next 3-5 years?

- If I need to customize it, can I?

- Do I need remote access to my system?

- Will I want to use it on multiple platforms?

- Do I foresee needing to share data with colleagues?

- Would I rather forget technology and use paper (no need to upgrade)?

- What is my budget?

- Does my institution provide any systems for free?

- Does my institution's IT department support it?

Finally, to reiterate an earlier essay, remember that the most important thing is to find a system that works for you, or find ways to work with the systems available to you, then commit to it. Choosing to change horses in midstream is a risky venture and not to be taken lightly. Because nobody wants to end up with a wet horse. Or rider.

Resources: Study Breaks and Personal Rewards

The Antediluvian Librarians would like to suggest these inexpensive and fat-free options for taking a break from your studies and/or rewarding yourself for your achievements along the way.

- Amble through a local exhibition

- Color with a 64-count pack of Crayons

- Do a charity walk/run

- Explore your campus/neighborhood/town

- Find a local farmer's market

- Get away from everyone and stare at nature

- Go on a picnic—if it's winter, make it a carpet picnic

- Play catch with a child . . . or a dog

- Kick off your shoes and go wading in a fountain or stream

- Meet a friend for coffee

- Plant some seeds

- Play Frisbee

- Read a beach book

- Re-watch a favorite movie or television show

- Ride a bike

- Spend the afternoon with a loved one

- Stay up late and look at the stars

- Take a drive somewhere you've never been

- Take a nap

- Take pictures of all your favorite people and places at school

- Take treats to your favorite elderly friend or relation

- Try a new recipe

- Visit a local attraction you've been too busy to check out

- Watch the ballgame with friends

- Window shop

Appendix: Homework

Take a few moments to explore the resources offered by your institution and its vicinity. Find answers to the following questions and enter the contact information into your mobile device.

Can you login to your school email account and have you set a password? Have you checked your email today?

Does your school have social media pages set up to provide news and information for incoming students? Have you joined them?

Where are the best places on and near your campus to get an inexpensive healthy meal?

Is there a campus clinic or health center you have access to?

Does your school or church offer counseling services? How can you access them?

What kinds of services—chair massages, therapy dog visits, yoga workshops—does your school offer at the end of term when exams and papers are coming due? If you school doesn't offer any, is there a student organization that might take on the project of organizing these services?

Does your library of campus IT department offer any resources or products to help you learn more efficiently and keep yourself organized? What are they?

How do you contact your campus IT department?

Specifically, does your institution provide access to text-to-speech software for converting your assigned readings to audio files?

Does your school offer wellness programs for students? Is there a campus gym?

Does your school publish a regular newsletter for students? Do you read it?

Where are three different locations at your school where you feel comfortable studying?

Where are the prettiest places to sit outside near your school and near your home?

What are your three favorite walks/jogs/bike rides around your school or home?

Which student organizations at your institution appeal to you the most? Is there an organization that does not exist that you might work to create?

What is the name and email address of your institution's reference librarian?

What are the hours that your library is open?

Have you walked the campus ahead of the semester to learn where your classes are being held?

What time is chapel? How often do they offer communion?

Who is your school's dean or president? If they sat next to you at lunch, would you recognize them?

Who is your academic advisor? What is their email?

Where can you park? How much will it cost?

Does your school offer any discounts for public transportation? This can be a good way to get some extra time for reading, studying, or napping

Does your school ID entitle you to any discounts at local businesses?

Where is the most convenient ATM? Post office? Photocopier? Scanner? Gas station? Pharmacy?

Acknowledgments

The basis of this work was a regular column in *Perkins News*, the newsletter for our community at Perkins School of Theology, Southern Methodist University, Dallas, Texas. At the behest of Assistant Dean of Student Life Tracy Anne Allred, Duane Harbin, and Jane Elder began the column in 2012 as a means of reaching students with information we hoped would help them with their work. David Schmersal joined us a bit later and continued until 2019, when a certain nameless Jezebel lured him away from our happy band to marry him. He is now enjoying a vastly enhanced domestic life in Austin, as well as a pretty great gig at the Austin Presbyterian Theological Seminary library.

The Antediluvian Librarians would not have had the temerity to turn these columns into a book without the encouragement of Anthony Elia, Director of Bridwell Library. We are honored that he chose to launch the Bridwell Library digital publication program with our work. Rebecca Howdeshell not only provided marvelous illustrations, but handled formatting, editing, digitizing, and design with her customary patience and panache. Leslie Fuller graciously agreed to apply her keen eye to proofreading and saved us from ourselves again and again. Classical history professor Melissa Barden Dowling contributed the Athena-like insights for which she is justly celebrated, thereby vastly improving our work. Members of the Bridwell Library Ink Tank, our reading and writing group, also participated in the editorial process; a special thanks goes out to members Richard Anastasi, Lillie Jenkins, Laura Figura, Michelle Ried, and Kay Smeal.

Finally, we want to express our appreciation and gratitude to the students of Perkins School of Theology, past and present, to whom this book is dedicated. You have made our professional lives delightful and fulfilling. Without your curiosity and good cheer, your engagement with your work, and your confidence in us, none of this would have been possible. We thank you all.

Printed in the USA
CPSIA information can be obtained
at www.ICGtesting.com
CBHW042100160924
14314CB00002B/2

9 781957 946016